CW01514129

SNOWFLAKE KISS

Edited by

Kelly Oliver

First published in Great Britain in 2002 by
ANCHOR BOOKS
Remus House,
Coltsfoot Drive,
Peterborough, PE2 9JX
Telephone (01733) 898102

All Rights Reserved

Copyright Contributors 2002

HB ISBN 1 85930 682 9
SB ISBN 1 85930 687 X

FOREWORD

Anchor Books is a small press, established in 1992, with the aim of promoting readable poetry to as wide an audience as possible.

We hope to establish an outlet for writers of poetry who may have struggled to see their work in print.

The poems presented here have been selected from many entries. Editing proved to be a difficult task and as the Editor, the final selection was mine.

I trust this selection will delight and please the authors and all those who enjoy reading poetry.

Kelly Oliver
Editor

CONTENTS

JENNY

When Jenny was born, no one was aware
That throughout her whole life
She would need medical care

She has lovely blue eyes, and light coloured hair
So contented and gentle
As she sits in her chair

Struck down with a syndrome that's extremely rare
Doctors unable to help her
Because there's no medical repair

Now 16 years old, it doesn't seem fair
But she's showered with love
By a family who care

One day at a time with a cross to bear
To keep her from suffering
Is all we ask in a prayer

Tom Rutherford

ON THE ROAD

On the road I met a man
We talked of many things
Miracles and mysteries
Vagabonds and kings

I bid him welcome to my house
We ate food and drank wine
He raised his hands upon high
And blessed the food and me and mine

But even then I could not see
Or recognise the man before me
But deep inside I knew
That I should know
His face, his name
The wounds upon his hands and feet

But he was gone again
Could it be, yes, yes, I cried
It was Jesus Christ, the son of God
Whom the Romans crucified.

L H Guest

THE INFANT JESUS

Oh infant Jesus
In a stable you were born
And the shepherds came to visit you,
Dressed in clothes all tattered and torn.
The sheep bleated softly, as you quietly slept
And into the stable I slowly crept.
Then I saw the three kings coming over the hill,
The night was so cold, dark and still.
But infant Jesus, no movement you made,
And the kings entered, heavily laden
With all the gifts which they gave.
They gave to you riches and gold,
I gave you nothing, but I kept you from the cold.
Oh infant Jesus
I was only young like you,
I crept into the stable, what else could I do?
I was only a small lamb
With a soft woolly fleece,
I knelt down beside you, while you slept at peace
And Mary and Joseph stroked my soft head
And they welcomed me with care,
And the shepherds and the kings
They all knelt in prayer, to praise God above
For your being there.

Trudie Sullivan

WORDS

Words can bring laughter,
Words can cause tears,
Words can magnify doubts or fears,
Take care how you use them,
Beware, they're not toys,
They are rough diamonds,
Not metal alloys.
Make them your friends, then,
Acknowledge their worth,
With just their assistance
You could conquer the earth!

Keith Allison

HOLY WINTER

The cold is everywhere,
Snow on the ground and on the rooftops around.
Days are short, nights are long,
Out of the bleakness a child was born,
On 25th December,
In a cattle shed,
In a manger,
On a night where a unique star shone bright.

It is a time for peace,
It is a special time of year,
Where some have nothing to spare,
So others with plenty share.
While some go about without a care.
A time for all kinds of holy spirits to be near.
A time for good will to all, to rear.

The son of God was born into our harshest of seasons
For the good of man was the reason
Because he was the one that was chosen.
Our Saviour to a kingdom to come
Entered by none but the wise, old and young.
So spread the faithful word by tongue,
For the promised land is where all the good belongs.
This is our most holiest of winter seasons.

Ali Sebastian

KYLE'S BAPTISM

Baby Kyle you are a sweetie
And you know it's true
We can never now imagine
The world without you.
With your smile so lovely
And your funny ways
You make us laugh and so you
Brighten up our days.

You are trusting us to be
All you need, so as you see
Us all trying to be fair
May your spirit with us share
Peace and joy your whole life through
Knowing God is calling you
To be bold and true and honest
Keeping all today has promised.

May you be the one who blesses
And helps clean up others' messes
As you find your place in life
As a peacemaker of strife
May this prophesy of mine
Be fulfilled, shine baby shine
You are here for special reasons
As you grow up through the seasons.

Never doubt we love you so
But someone loves you more I know
That one is Jesus and because he's real
You will be blessed his love to feel
This poem is in knowledge you
Will be as nice your whole life through.

Phyllis Shotton

JUST A THOUGHT AWAY

I had a dream of a wonderful place,
Where every creed and every race,
Lived in harmony one with another,
Black and white, just like sister and brother.
A most beautiful place filled with peace and love,
Tranquillity and accord of the peaceful dove.
Imagine lion and lamb both laying together,
Living in harmony for ever and ever.
A dream is only a thought away,
Today, tomorrow and every day.

Zolyar

A FRIEND IN GOD

In God I have a friend
He takes me to the rainbow's end
Lets me sing his own sweet song
Keeps me safe and I am never wrong

In God I have a good pal
The stormiest sea together we sail
I am safe in his golden boat
He shows me how not to gloat

In God I have my best mate
He leads me to see the pearly gate
I find my home with Saint Peter
In Heaven where the water is sweeter

In God I find a real buddy
He gives me my lesson to study
I can walk with him for ages
My past mistakes fill a full page

In God we have more than a chum
He is with our family in Kingdom come
He takes care of all our strife
Leads us to his eternal life.

Colin Allsop

MYSTERY SOLVED

I tried to visualise the world,
When I'm no longer here,
Instead, I saw the bitter truth,
So staggeringly clear,
My world is mine, and mine alone,
With its heaven and its hell,
It's in my head, so when I'm dead,
It will be dead as well.

Matthew L Burns

WE YIELD

We yield our hands
In service, Lord, for Thee.
Now, by Your power,
Your hands they shall be.

We yield our feet,
Our pathways we present;
Now they are Yours,
To cross each continent.

We yield our lips
To honour You our King;
Our voices now, Lord,
To Your praise we bring.

We yield our knees,
That they would bow in prayer.
We yield our shoulders,
Fit to burdens bear.

Our hands, our feet,
Our lips, our all is Thine;
Instruments of
Your righteousness divine.

Ken Millar

Mummy

No one to hold me and tell me they care.
No one to love me and say they will be there.
No one to call me mummy and say don't cry.
I will close my eyes and picture Jesus high above.
I hope that he will show me love.

Sylvia Brown

THE FIFTH ANGEL

With infinite clamouring, golden wings,
As if a venomous army fighting,
Harangued within, blazing, lightning
Feathers, fifth angel, before the rings
Of the six immortal chords, sings,
Joy, flies out, and an immortal, biting,
Star, bright, does fall, descends from righting
Heaven unto mortal oceans flings
Onto pastures green and pleasant, Earth,
Tragic in honour and glory to weep:
Presented to the Lord's fifth angel mirth
That blasphemous unseen key of the deep
That never-ending black hole all rending
Abaddon's horrendous hell descending.

Edmund Saint George Mooney

THE FUTURE

Mobile phones
Faxes to please
Communication
No longer seized

Letters through post
No longer the aim
As e-mails are sent
Instead of the same

Robots as pets
The future
May be
Soon to be vexed

Digital TV
Phone with a camera
For all to see
Soon will be the key

The future is ours
To do as we wish
Technology changes
What next on the list?

Kristina Howells

FAIRYTALE

As the orchestra strikes up a tune
She glides across the darkened room;
Round and round in the fearsome embrace
Of a malevolent stranger with a grin on his face.
She follows his lead, she avoids his eyes
As the sound of the music covers her cries.
Imprisoned within these four cold walls,
Besieged by ogres, spirits and trolls,
This beautiful princess locked up in her tower
As her partner dances her, hour after hour.
He spins her round and round and round
Her feet now barely touch the ground.
As they dance together in concentric rings,
Faster than a hummingbird's wings,
She sees from the corners of her vision
Other couples dance with precision.
Their moves are measured, their step is light
As though, to them, this speed feels right.
Some smile and laugh and seem at ease
While others echo her own pleas
And as the music now begins slowing
She understands just where she's going.
Alongside everyone in this room
She has been dancing to her final tune
And though she's tired now; out of breath,
She keeps on dancing; dancing with death
And in her heart she knows its over -
She has no prince prepared to save her.
She tries to stop, but to no avail
In her real-life nightmare fairytale.

Suie Nettle

BERTHA CHILDS

Bertha Childs ran all the way
Home, ran and ran until
The door banged shut behind
Her small behind.

She could not possibly tell
Her mater what a dreadful
Fate nearly befell her;
Only her pillow pillowed her sighs.

She had recently learnt to dance,
But how she danced, without the faintest
Notion that dance was the spoon
To stir and administer love's potion.

Something which held heavily in
The air that night had tangled
In her hair; she saw his eyes roll
Bright, felt his hands were fire brands.

New, unborn, unshared, willing lust
Flared up, exsufflicate, in her
Woman glands; she saw his eyes roll
Bright, felt his hands were fire brands.

Bertha Childs ran all the way home
Ran and ran until
The door banged shut behind
Her small behind.

Robert Wynn-Davies

A FRIEND

Ever feel needed as a friend?
Something inside says I need to bend.
Can I ever take on board needs of others,
Feel their wants, time to spend.
Think about what it means once I start,
Sharing thoughts, worries, a trend.
Relief comes, sometimes tears!
Emotion overflows, not meant to offend.
Hugs will follow, gratitude on show!
Now I know a friend, yes, a friend!

John Mann

THE SNEEZE

There are lots of peculiar things in life,
And one is that of sneezing.
For some it can be annoying,
And for some it can be pleasing.
An itch can simply make you sneeze,
And bright light might start you off,
Maybe you don't sneeze at all,
Some people sneeze and cough.
Sneezing can be enjoyable,
Some hate it altogether,
An awful lot have sneezing fits
That's caused by windy weather.
Some may sneeze when down with flu
From the mucus up their noses.
It is possible to sneeze on purpose
Just from sniffing roses.
Then there are those who sneeze for fun,
By tickling their nostril hair.
Some will sneeze not noticing,
Because simply they don't care.
It may be you sneeze in your sleep,
While dreaming of a sneeze.
Maybe you are really weird
And sneeze when sniffing cheese.
Sneezing is a fact of life,
But make sure when you sneeze;
Hold your hands up to your mouth
Or put your head between your knees.

Christopher Penhale

LOVE AND LIFE, THE KEYS

Of all things that we respect in life
Some words are supreme and can ease our strife
Serenity and peace can calm troubled time
And through them a perfect peace can be thine.

At times we succumb to mortal greed
Take more than an animal needs to feed
Though we know it's wrong and hesitate
The foul deed is done before we wait.

As man is by no means perfect yet
Understanding he seeks, the truth to get
Deep love within, misunderstanding sometimes
Blurs faith as one struggles with unrehearsed lines

Modern times encourage man to lapse into sin
False reasoning, untruths, goad man from within
A time to be strong, know what is right, do your best
Man must stand firm as he goes through life's tests.

The key is respect for all and their kin
Devotion and humility, both come from within
Adoration and fondness entwine side by side
With belief and true love the inspirational guide.

We are born with the truth inside us as began
The continuance of life as conceived by woman and man
As one travels life's path, trying to understand why
Somewhere comes a strength that helps you get by.

Though sometimes alone, alone can't be real
With so many so near, just like you, can't you feel
Inner warmth emits and encapsulates like forms
Instigates life like days are precluded by dawns.

Take stock, breathe deep, look into her eyes
Her pools of light will tell you no lies
Look deep within, honesty can be seen
It is her, only her, for you the king, your queen.

Tony W Rylatt

MONEY TO WASTE

People drinking spirits, or maybe beer
Does it make them happy, bringing them cheer?
Others smoking cigarettes by the pack
They're short of something they think they don't lack
Folk ringing silly phone lines for a chat
Why do it? What's the point in that?
Some get involved in organised crime
Isn't it the age we called time?
A few going to casinos or betting shops
How do they know when to stop?
Why do some mess about with call girls
Seduction and desire puts their head in a swirl
None of this is quite to my taste
That's because I've no money to waste

P Edwards

LORD, I'M BLESSED

Twice my life has been so blessed
with all the love and happiness
that having a baby brings our way,
their presence in our lives each day.

As each day passes, bigger they grow,
they learn at speed and then they know
exactly how to get their way,
whatever I try to do or say.

First words are followed by first steps -
all their progress I gladly accept
till they answer back and run away,
causing my voice and nerves to fray.

My stress is not an office thing,
I get it from my two offspring!
They run me ragged, make me shout,
then ask, 'What are you cross about?'

When at last we turn out the light,
having exchanged a kiss goodnight,
this is when we all can rest
and I remember, 'Lord, I'm blessed.'

Andrea Sandford

MY LOVE

To others it's just youth when I explain my love,
Laughable I see us together,
For the unseeable future you're my partner,
For infinity, I'm planning forever.
The overwhelming loss when we're apart
And our reunion brings every smile.
Seems foolish to the lonely
For they can only mock and beguile.
But the bond we've forged goes deeper
To a level of the heart unexplored,
Hidden from the past
As their probing was ignored.
But I open up to you
And need for you to know.
That this love is pure and honest,
Affection that can only grow.
For the days we have each other,
Night's memories keep you here,
And the time that we have shared
Bring our strength and future near.

Hayley Beddoes

FREEDOM CRUSADE

'Who would care to join me
On a freedom day?' she cried.
'We could pack ourselves a picnic
And go out for a ride.'

The three looked at each other,
Their faces shone with glee.
'Can we go on an adventure?
Take a journey by the sea?'

So early one bright morning,
They all set out at last.
This would be a special day
For the magic had been cast.

They drove down to the ocean,
Walked the pebbles on the shore.
Each had a different story,
Of the wonders that they saw.

One became an eagle
Soaring high into the sky.
Another Pochohontis
Her spirit free to fly.

The third became a druid
In a circle made of stone.
I, well I rejoiced in watching them,
And then I took them home.

Megan Fitz-Patrick

THE WHEEL OF LIFE

Life is a journey, right through the years
From birth until death, through so many tears
Life is a journey, that brings you so near
Through so many stages, through rules to adhere
Life is a journey with only one way
Through so many problems, to get through each day
Life is a journey with only one way
With so many fears for each brand new day
Life is a journey that keeps us all going
Life is a wheel without ever knowing.

Paula Doyle

Coco

He lived next door when just a kitten
And had a coat of chocolate brown.
He was one of eight, but I was smitten
Whenever he came around.
He'd visit with his sister
Who was black and white.
Although none of them were related,
As the eldest, he kept them right.
His name was Coco, and as he grew
All circumstances changed.
His owners had to give up the cats
And further afield they ranged.
I was offered to choose one
And Coco was the one for me.
He hadn't been cared for properly,
Now he was happy - plain to see.
Coco paid me back immensely
With gifts galore and more.
With dormice, voles and fieldmice
And sparrows by the score.
His most extravagant present
Was a big, fat, juicy worm
Even just to think of it
Makes my body squirm.
Still, in spite of all the killing,
I love him - without excuse.
He's fluffy, friendly and funny,
Our lovely family puss.

Evelyn Osman

A TIME FOR RHYME

Wintertime, cold, cold snow
Freezing fog - and spirits low

Summertime, sun so hot
Green, green leaves - forget-me-nots

Summer, winter, cold or hot
We'd still all be wishing that it is what it's not!

H Hyde

CHRISTMAS CHEER

Children's faces all aglow
What's going to happen? No one knows
Playing and shouting in the snow
Tobogganing down the hills they go
Snowball throwing to and fro.

It's Christmas soon, Santa's letters to write
What to ask for on Christmas night
A dress for Mum, a razor for Dad
Two new bones for Thomas and Tad
A train for Peter, ballet shoes for me
And lots and lots of more goodies.

The tree's going up, decorations around
The house looks like a fairyland
Friends to call, parties to have
A great time by all was had
It's off to bed we hear Mum cry
Or Santa's going to pass you by.

Up we go with good intention
To stay awake in anticipation
Yet, falling asleep still Christmas is here
House full of goodies and lots of cheer
We've had a great time, the day has passed
And now it's off to bed at last.

Shoshanna Fletcher

BEAUTY OF THE DALES

In late October where can we go?
The leaves are falling and it could even snow
So off we went through the villages, one by one
Saw Bolton Castle with the sun shining on.

The trees looked lovely in shades of bronze, yellow and green
Many fields were bare, not like they used to be,
It's foot and mouth which has taken its toll
But many of the farmers look ready to start and go.

Over the moors we travelled to the village of Dent
It was shrouded in mist with the roads looking bent,
A hawk on the wall looked ready to pounce
For something to eat such as a bird or a mouse.

The sun came through as we arrived back at the station
It's the highest in England so it was an occasion
To take pictures to remember our day out in October
Before winter creeps in and the leaves would be over.

Looking down from the hill were a group of shooters
Saw many grouse who were making sounds like hooters
Some were bobbing here and there among the heather
We were praying that their lives would be spared forever.

On our journey back we travelled down the dale
The mist had dispersed and some trees looked pale,
Over the butter tubs we ventured to see
Swaledale full of beauty which it will always be.

Bessie Metcalfe

CHILDREN LIKE GODS

The water always washed away the sands
when we built castles on the beach. We made
worlds which slipped silently out of our hands
as tides came in and out. We laughed and played

when we built castles on the beach. We made
valleys and mountain ranges, streams which flowed
as tides came in and out. We laughed and played
like thoughtless little gods; we bravely strode

valleys and mountain ranges, streams which flowed
until we trod them flat. We never saw,
like thoughtless little gods - we bravely strode
across the lands that we would see no more

because we trod them flat. We never saw
worlds which slipped silently out of our hands:
and from the lands that we would see no more
the water ever washed away the sands.

Dylan Pugh

TROUBLE ABROAD

Miami airport, full of bustle,
good looking men with plenty of muscle,
a cab approached, full of holes,
first impressions, angry souls.
Hotel doors bolted and barred,
memories linger, forever scarred,
elegantly perched, sipping a Coke,
suddenly surrounded by serious folk,
rifles were pointing from roofs up above,
the thief next to me was not someone to love.
He left the scene without any force,
holidays abroad, all par for the course.
When a karate instructor, early twenties,
flew into the lounge, totally demented,
had been mugged on the street whilst taking a walk,
gave rise for concern and a reason to talk,
safety in numbers, for the rest of the stay,
enough troubles at home, without having to pay.

B J Harrison

THE FUTURE

Your future lies ahead of you
Like a field of pure white snow
You must tread it carefully
As on life's path you go

Your past now lies behind you
Like a field of new-mown hay
Don't let it lie and wither
Don't let it waste away

Remember all the happy times
But don't forget the tears
They are part of life's rich pattern
As you go from year to year

Keep striving for a better life
However long it takes
By looking back into your past
To learn from your mistakes

Now face the future with a smile
And you will surely find
That you will be remembered
As credit to mankind

Aileen Anderson

BONE IDOL

This is a comfortable place you may be sure
For it's very, very seldom that I lay on the floor,
The back of the settee is where I elegantly sprawl
And there's tons of cushions if I should fall.

When my master gets up to leave the room
Into his nice warm chair I quickly zoom,
There's also a chair with cushions just right
Where I can sit and watch the TV all night.

What's that I see? It's got me very excited
Another dog in my house - it's got to be righted
I'll run up to it and bark as loud as can be,
Look, there it's gone - I've looked behind the TV.

There's that tune again, oh! and there's that cat,
My mistress says it's 'Coronation Street' - I'm not sure about that,
There's lots of silly people running after a ball,
I really can't understand why at all.

The garden's so large with good places to sniff around,
My master says I'm like a Hoover with nose on the ground,
He's built a platform by the fence for me to see
All the dogs and people I can bark at excitedly.

I've been walked, fed and watered again today
It really is quite a good place to stay,
Now my master's stood up and 'Right!' he's just said,
I know that's the word - we're going to bed.

Sylvia Olliver

GOOD NEWS

Good news we have to tell today
Good news we told just yesterday
Tomorrow's news will be good too
News so exciting and it's true
It's *Jesus is alive and well*
No greater news is there to tell
It's news that through the world has spread
For *Jesus is alive not dead.*

Royston Davies

LET IMAGINATION FLOW

Close your eyes
What do you see?
Use your imagination
Where would you like to be?
In your mind's eye
You can be anywhere, be anyone
Don't be too serious
Do it, just for fun

Relax, let imagination flow
Beautiful gardens, sunshine
A golden yellow sunset.
Holding a glass of your favourite wine
As you use your imagination
Let a smile form on your lips.
You're dancing a waltz
Gently swaying your hips.

For a brief moment in time
Your imagination flows
Dream yourself into another world
Away from your cares and woes.

Then, gradually open your eyes
Come slowly back down to earth
Allowing imagination to flow
Is a gift given at birth
You can be anywhere, be anyone
Don't be too serious
Do it just for fun.

Anne Logan

POETIC STYLE

I like my poetry simple and clear;
Straight from the heart, easy on the ear,
Words in daily use, those I know,
Telling tales of glee and a few of woe

I don't want to refer to a lexicon to reveal the message;
I like to feel the impact from each individual passage.
Directly, poignantly, excitedly, explicitly and wholeheartedly too,
Leaving me in no doubt as to what I should construe.

Allen Jessop

WHY

When my daddy went away
We didn't say goodbye
I knew he had been very ill
I didn't know that he would die

The angels crept into his room
When he slept one night
Then they very gently
Took him into the light

Now he's on a journey to
A spiritual, happy place
I never ever will forget
His happy, smiling face

Although he's gone forever
And I won't see him again
I will always miss him but
I'm glad he'll have no pain

My daddy's up in Heaven
In a new home, I believe
I still don't understand
Why he had to leave.

Keena

HAS GOD EVER SPOKEN TO YOU?

In the quiet of the morning,
In the rush of the day.
As you drive in your car,
In your work or your play.

Has God ever spoken to you?

In your routine of worship.
In the pattern of things.
Have you ever stopped and listened
To the words that He brings?

Or have you continued in ways that you know.
Turned a blind eye to emotions that show.
Or condemned those who tell for being absurd.
'It can't possibly happen - it's not God they heard!'

But stop and take stock and open your mind.
Don't judge and don't mock, that's being unkind.
Take time to listen and open your heart
For there's a message for us God wants to impart.

We have to move forward, revive and renew.
We cannot stay still, God's work is to do.
To remain as we are we will only stagnate.
To encourage new followers could be too late.

When we have moved onward, what will be left?
Empty church buildings in ruins, bereft!
Or happy, young people who gather in joy,
Who'll go out in the world their gifts to employ.

We've got to have faith and we will progress.
For God will guide us out of this mess.
Don't be afraid of the future we see
For believe it or not, God has spoken to me.

Sue Ireland

A TIME FOR RHYME

Free verse I name 'poetic prose'
Its authors deem that 'anything goes'
If words, though pretty, lack a frame
Their so-called 'poem' is just a game
To baffle poetry lovers, who
Enjoy a 'mental dance' - it's true
'Cos words are music word-designed
So, rhyme and rhythm must be defined
Like symphony, étude, motet
When if the notes on sheets are set
In clefs and bars within the 'score'
Plus regular beats - 2, 3, or 4.
Such 'melodies' like free verse 'art'
Might be off-putting from the start
So, for the sake of verse for those
Who'll choose to stick to poems - or prose
Give place to rhyming rhythmic lines
Together their delight entwines
Both joy plus mental music too
And leave free verse to erudite few.

Frances Cox

LAKES AND FELLS

White clouds casting shadows on green and purple fells,
Walkers climbing steadily along the ridges of Cat Bells.
Clear streams gurgling gaily down toward the lakes,
Breathtaking beauty surrounds us, and within us wakes,
Alerts us to the wonder and the beauty that abounds,
Lifting up our senses to enjoy the sights and sounds,
As shadows slowly deepening, turns blue sky to dark red,
Bringing on the sunset and it's then we homeward head,
We soak our weary bodies in water, soothing, hot,
And later, quietly dining, we discuss whether or not,
To next day walk a valley, or climb another fell,
But tomorrow is another day and which of us can tell,
We only know we like the sound as boots strike lakeland stone,
And in this part of the country, you are never quite alone,
There's camaradie in the way that walkers share their tales,
About their own experiences of walking in the dales,
And later, when we've left the fells and returned to where we live,
The memories of our walks and climbs so much pleasure give,
And we look forward to the day when once more we will go,
Among the fells and placid lakes and once again to know,
That this part of the country is made of stone, and cloud, and rain,
A place of timeless beauty, we'll return to many times again.

Eileen Cuddy Buckley

SONNET TO DOROTHY

Why is my mind filled with such tender thoughts,
I see your face, when you are not with me,
As if the sun was locked within my soul,
And you, and you alone, now hold the key.

What fills my chest so that I scarce can breathe,
And soft emotions feel where'er I go,
I feel the warmth of love that your glance brings,
As year by year my love for thee doth grow.

I cannot think of what life might have been,
Had we not met so many years ago,
Although to me it seems but yesterday,
That seeds of love did first in my heart grow.

But time doth fly, and fifty years have fled,
Since we held hands and waited to be wed . . .

John Whittock

OBITUARY OF A HAPPY COUPLE

Mourn not that your parents have gone at last
More than 80 happy years they passed
They lived life to the full.
Memories kept them from feeling dull
Many things they've done together
Like walking in fine or stormy weather
Swimming in the cold, rough sea
Tho' that was more for me than he,
On a boat he'd rather be
But that was too confined for me.
To our next adventure we've moved on
Together, hand in hand as one.

Alice Hall

TIME FOR RHYME

Writing in rhyme is a pleasure
One I enjoy to the full!
Though it needs a good deal of leisure
To find the right words, that will pull
The reader into the picture,
You're trying so hard to create.
A notebook, and den, are a fixture,
Any time, day, night or bedmate.
An eye, always on the lookout,
Or, an ear, tuned to pick up the sound
Of things of interest, to write about.
Inspiration, your greatest need.
The will to put into verse.
So much time and effort to weed out,
Make changes, sometimes curse.
When the lines don't seem to please you -
When the theme seems to be all wrong,
Then, that's the time for you to re-do
It, make it up as you go along.

Winifred Swann

CHRISTMAS TIME

Our four sons come home for Christmas
Every single year,
It's so wonderful to have them back
The family is complete when they are here.
Our boys have all now scattered
As they are grown-up young men
So we don't all get together often
Though we get calls and visits now and then.
At Christmas it is like the old days
The noisy chatter while they eat their fill,
We all reminisce about their childhood
And they laugh and tease each other still.
Now I really hate it on Boxing Day
When the last one goes I feel so sad
The house feels too quiet and empty
The only ones left are me and their dad.
As so much can happen in a year
Until we're all together once more
We have decided to join the high-tech age
So we can all send e-mails by the score.
This is a really modern convenience
Like our dependency on the mobile phone,
To let folk know exactly where we are
When we're comin' or where we're goin'.
However, nothing compares to human contact
A smile, a big hug or a kiss,
Each year we have many more memories to add
When we take the time to reminisce.

Mary Anne Scott

ALMOST THERE

The lights switched off
But there's a glow
Around the room
The shadows grow.

A crackle in the hearth
Like a shot
Excitement mounting
The sound of the clock.

Heavy-eyed and full
Of wonder
Little people
Short on slumber.

Discarded crisp wrappers
And a jellybean pack
Santa's supper piled neatly
By the chimney stack.

Colourful stockings dangling
From the mantelpiece
A background carol
Newly released.

A break in the silence
Like a crunch in the snow
Anticipation mounting
One minute to go.

Gloria Hargreaves

THE CARS THAT DISAPPEARED

If you go to Saunton Sands and dig down in the burrows -
you will find vintage cars, packed in ordered furrows.

Daimlers, Dodges, Buicks, Fords - all spanking, sparkling new;
just waiting 'neath the shifting dunes - long lost to public view.

The secret is that long ago, in August thirty-one -
we'd all gone to spend the day, with sand and sea and sun.

Aged only four, I'd brought my cars to play with by the sea;
all went well until there came my mother's call for tea.

To keep them safe I'd covered them with a layer of sand -
before going off to munch away the sandwich in my hand.

On my return I dug in vain, as more and more I feared
the awful truth that, whilst at tea, my cars had disappeared.

Winds had blown; seas had roared; sand had spiralled and swirled -
settling again in patterns and forms of a totally different world.

That's how Devon's Saunton Sands left a lifetime's scars
on a little boy who never found - where he'd left his cars.

Edward Fursdon

BEER, BEER, BEER

When I was young and in my prime
you couldn't kiss me
for a pound a time
please more beer, more wine
believe you-me, now I feel fine
now I am old and growing stale
believe me my serving wench, come here me darlin'
this here flagon, the beer I'm slowly slurping down
what's that for, this old yokel, a crown
get this here beer down me, my price is only
half an ale.

Jonathan Covington

OUR LOVE

You say you love me so
now's the time to let it show
or you, my love, will have to go
do you love me so?

I want to know you care
your feelings you will not share
I'm in despair
do you really care?

Can't take anymore
don't want a war
but you just closed the door
on my love once more.

S Shakesby

WERE I

Were I to turn and walk away
And venture from your sight,
Would your heart grow heavy
As you faced the lonely night?

Were I to run and take your heart
Could you withstand the pain,
And if I made you sorely hurt
Could you take me back again?

Were I to say the cruellest things
With words that were unkind,
Would you accept my 'sorry'
Forgiveness could you find?

These things I pray that you would do
If I should tend to stray,
For all these things I'd do for you
Almost every waking day.

Duchess Newman

THIS FUNNY OLD WORLD

'It's a funny old world,' said the man to his wife,
'Where we toil and we work for most of our lives,
And we pay into this, and we pay into that:
Only to find we must beg for some back!'

'It's a funny old world,' said the wife to her man,
'Where we count every penny, and do what we can
To make both ends meet, but the worries persist
As bills keep arriving and savings grow less.'

'It's a funny old world,' said the man to his son,
'Where progress is made yet we're no further on.
The pauper still begs and the homeless still squat,
And the wars keep on raging: unable to stop!'

'It's a funny old world,' said the son to the corpse,
As he stood in the chapel and cried for his da,
'Where we struggle through daily and fight to survive,
Yet, once we give in we find peace of mind!'

Sandra Wolfe

CINDY

Underneath the rosemary bush when it's sunny to be in the shade
Never likes to see intruders on her patch, whoever approaches
Is warned away from her special place of sanctuary.
If they were to return it would be at their cost.
It is deemed to be her property.

'The aroma is superb and the solitude is great
Wish I could stay for dinner on my very fancy plate
Why do I have to go inside and meet with all the fuss?
I know when it's time to feed myself, I shouldn't have to rush.

When I go indoors I hide away from those who wish

                                                    to fondle me.
Independence I prefer, I'm getting on a bit you see.
I've had a good life - cannot grumble - with folk who really care for me.
All the same I still prefer to be under the bush of the rosemary.'

Iris Wagstaff

Seasons

Spring opens its sleepy eyes
From winter's clutch releases the ties
Bows to the sun in adoration
While coming out of hibernation

Trees endow themselves with bud
Crocuses show above the mud
Bluebells in abundance grow
And daffs and tulips stage their show

Birds twitter on bough and bush
While making nests they shove and push
They can't ignore their inborne drive
For having young and staying alive

The joy of spring and winter's death
The air is pure upon the breath
The birth of flowers, sweetly scented
Nobody mourns the passing of the late lamented.

James Valentine Sullivan

FARCE

Bombing, fighting and killing daily,
With shelling the instant response,
Here we recycle with enthusiasm weekly,
Regulated emissions soon to ensconce.

Bombing, fighting and killing daily,
Villages smashed by the carpet bomb,
We use smoke-free fuels oh! so cleanly,
Menace of the fridge stressed upon.

Bombing, fighting and killing daily,
Starving refugees now on the run,
In this world there is no equality,
In the west we have food by the ton.

Bombing, fighting and killing daily,
'No damage', the fundamentalists con,
Britain has multiple brands of each commodity,
With every exotic cuisine laid on.

Bombing, fighting and killing daily,
Threats of a wicked nuclear reply,
Birds and animals watched by us closely,
To save from extinction? We really must try.

Bombing, fighting and killing daily,
Pictures sent across the world in a flash,
So common, we become numb to the brutality,
Acutely grim this bloody dash.

Bombing, fighting and killing daily,
Women swathed in the burqa from head to toe,
This is the ultimate repressive accessory,
Unbelievable that medieval indoctrined foe.

Mercy Jackson

COUNT YOUR BLESSINGS

I can't believe you're gone my love,
I can't believe you're gone,
That you're not in the world my love,
And I am all alone.

My mind is full of memories,
Of lovely times gone by,
My heart is full of you, my love,
Why have you gone - oh why?

But I really can't complain,
I found that love was true,
You brightened every day, my love,
My happiness was you.

So I must learn to live each day,
I'm really not alone,
For even though you've gone, my love,
I'm still a lucky *mum*.

D M Carne

MY LIFE

My life is like a picture book, eager to begin
I hurtle through the early pages, never stopping to think,
Of other people's feelings I may trample on the way
Or that, one day there may be a price to pay.

The early scenes in black and white, images of long ago,
My parents, two people, I never really got to know.
Their love, a protective shell, I felt they didn't care,
In trying to understand, emotions are laid bare.

Colour brightens the pages as we move to present day,
Absent from my life those restrictive shades of grey.
Maturity brings new perspective on my early years of life;
Busy mother of three children, a devoted, loving wife.

Time has flown so quickly, too late to change the past,
I sift through precious memories to find foundations solidly cast.
Only now I appreciate the love that surrounded me before;
As past and present merge into one, my heart takes flight, to soar.

Half way through my book of life, there is still so much to learn,
Right from wrong and good from bad are no easier to discern;
With confidence I look ahead to a future bright with dreams,
Love, the precious constant, ageless and evergreen.

Karen Davies

THE BAKER'S DOZEN

Bill Baker was an awful dunce
His arithmetic was bad
His classmates said he was a fool
His future seemed so sad.
Then someone had a great idea
The cookery class might do
So Billy joined up with the girls
And donned an apron too.
His teacher there was most impressed
He gained the highest grade
His cakes and bread scored such acclaim
He sold each one he made.
Bill Baker, now, had found his nitch
Baker by trade and name
He baked all day - sometimes at night
And blossomed in his fame.
His counting never did improve
His pies no one could beat,
And no one minded his mistakes
It meant one more to eat.
The baker's dozen is no myth
Here's how it all began
That extra one was good for trade
Now Bill's a wealthy man.

Elsie Sharman

My Testing Days

Flat land and raised roadways where you can see for miles,
Yet fortunately you can't look back and remember what was vile.
You're too far gone. No wind will push you there - unless God says,
And I don't think he'd let that be. You've had your testing days.
But who am I to read his mind? Can I predict torment?
Can I know how I will cope in times of turbulence?
I've lots to learn, and years to come. (I hope) I'm ignorant still,
All my others (brothers, sisters) struggle, so I probably will.

The one thing I am certain of (if anything's that clear-cut)
(History has this catalogued and written-up and shut.)
I could be one of the crowd, and suffocate my faith,
Heeding through withdrawal signs, in time to resuscitate.
Safer hence to force-march on, to strengthen through the storm,
When though the tempest rages fast, the Christian soldiers on,
For we are in a holy war, though we like to call for peace
(Which never lasts, nay, never starts, like an empty-tabled feast).

So push the doors and be prepared in every season's wake,
And keep it going both for yourself and others' future sake.
Familiarity breeds contempt. I wish it wasn't true.
I can't deny it's happening in me and possibly you.
How many teachings do you dilute, subtly, subconsciously?
And how different (for the worse) are you in purity?
From a few generations back from now? Go. Add up the change.
Know once we stood firm. Demanded respect. Now we're seen
                                                    as a deranged.

Andrew Sanders

LET NO MAN CALL ME HONEY

Oh how sweet the melody be
The song you are singing just for me
It breaks my heart to hear you say
That soon you'll be going far away
Why did you love me then break my heart?
You said we'd never be apart
You lied to me, were you ever true
Or was I just another in the queue?
Oh! Feckless man in my life destroyed
Now you leave me real annoyed
No! I shall not sigh and weep
Into a new life I shall leap
I'll guard my heart and never more
Shall callous man my heart explore
I'll enjoy my life and spend my money
God help the next man who calls *me* Honey.

June Clare

A TIME FOR RHYME

'I couldn't be bothered' is a phrase you hear
From older folk who are, I fear
Giving way to a lazy frame of mind
And think that cleaning is a bind!

They may, some time, a duster flick
And moan that they are feeling sick
So on the bed they go and lie
And watch the birds up in the sky.

The shopping, too, has to be done
To order by the phone's more fun
Than pushing a trolley round the store
And buying useless goods galore.

In a copper you washed in olden days
Too busy to sit about and laze -
The iron was put on the gas stove heat
And clothes were pressed and looked so neat

But now, an electric iron's the thing
So, 'I couldn't be bothered' has lost its sting
What do we do with all the spare times?
We sit down and write a poem that rhymes!

Inez Henson

CHOOSE YOU

God's gathering His people, for the battle has begun,
Jesus is the captain, God's great and mighty Son,
He will lead and we must follow, come, fall in step behind,
He's a strong, trustworthy leader and His discipline is kind.
In this the last great battle, everyone must take a stand,
No special skills are needed as in His strength we go,
He fills us with His courage to fight against the foe.
Or do you fight for Satan? Make the choice my friend,
The battle's now in progress, the chance won't come again.

Alan Ellsmore

NIGHT AND DAY

The night seems permanent like death
yet its haunting blankness will succumb,
and the stars will lose their timid haze,
once the day's first hour has come.

Lead on then daylight, guide the way,
your brilliance heaven sent;
show us the meaning of the day
before our light is spent.

Susan Turner

A JUNGLE BEAUTY

This jungle beauty hides in trees
Enjoys the sun and gentle breeze
But only size can bring her fame
For anaconda's not a dame.

H Atkinson

MONKEY BUSINESS

As one chimp to another my pal today I ail
'Whatever is wrong? Might I enquire?'
'Yes, I have a twist in my tail.'
'How did this happen? It looks painful I admit.'
'I looped the loop up in a tree and got myself in a fix.
My tail was there for balance, correct me if I am wrong,
As I hurled myself from branch to branch I swung merrily along.
Then all of a sudden, to dodge a nest of bees,
I had to make a detour and was not very pleased.
And that is when it happened, as I swung with all my might,
My tail was curled around a branch and held me fast and tight.
I pulled and tugged and here is the consequence, on view for all to see,
There is a permanent twist in my lovely tail that was once

a pride to me.'
'Cheer up, it could have been worse, with no tail at all,
Then you would have come to grief in an undignified fall.
I know you love to swing up high and reach the very top,
Time will heal, as you reveal, it's rather cute your corkscrew flop.'
'Not appreciating your sense of humour, I must go and hide,
To seek some form of medication, hopingly this poor tail will survive.'
Visiting a wise old monkey who gave advice for free,
He gently unravelled that chimp's lovely tail then bound it tightly.
The tail improved and is usable, as again his happiness reigns,
That chimp is joined by his own clan, they admire his prehensile range.
They chatter and they clatter amongst those treetops high,
This chimp's now extra careful and slower movements are now applied.

R Hiscoke

THE WAITING GAME

I crouch and lap the milk in the bowl
while covertly watching the little, dark hole
over there, in the skirting board, under the window
a twitch of the tail and I'm ready to go
my ears attuned for the slightest sound
swivelling, travelling all around
whiskers a-twitching, vibrating, seeking
a movement, a touch, a physical feeling
nose a-searching for a smell
sniffing, snuffling, all is well
paws resting quietly upon the floor
ready to spring into action once more
body quivering, fur pricked up high
adrenaline pumping, I'm ready to fly
all is quiet - but wait - there's a rustle
soon now there's going to be hustle and bustle
muscles tensed and crouched down low
it's very nearly time to go
whiskers taught, ears are still
nose stopped twitching - smell and kill
a shadow appears upon the wall
the game is on, no time to stall . . .

I scutter, scatter to the little dark hole
and watch as a cat lands in the bowl
with a hiss he knows he's missed his prey
as this little mouse lives to see another day.

Dino Carlin

ALICE AT THE BARBER'S

I'm in an operation gown
But not on a table
Just a chair
With a rest
For my feet.

I don't feel a thing
But there's no needle
Just a comb
And a brush
In my hair.

The instruments are sharp
But they move in a
Scissoring,
Smoothing way
Round my ears.

The power is switched on
But there's no danger
Only a hum
Which nibbles
At my neck.

And I can see the whole operation
But only, of course, through a looking-glass.

Glen Pride

SEVENTEEN

Childhood days are past.
Just where have they been?
The years have rolled on fast.
He is seventeen!

Gone is childish prattle.
Gone the nursery rhymes.
Gone his baby rattle
with the lulling chimes.

Teddy lies in a cupboard
where he can't be seen,
with 'Tales Of Mother Hubbard',
he is seventeen!

With boyhood days left behind,
he can hardly wait,
at seventeen, true love to find,
with her, his special date.

The time has come, she is there.
Firm, sleek body, clad in red.
His heart flutters all astir.
He runs towards her, words unsaid.

Her closeness near, he shows emotion.
This is his best day by far.
He will treat her with true devotion.
He's seventeen and has his very own car.

Josie Rawson

LITTLE ANGEL

I am a little angel,
I have two little wings,
I have a golden harp
with little golden strings.
I sit upon my cloud
playing songs all day,
and I do it all for nothing,
I don't even ask for pay.
With blonde, curly hair,
and little pink cheeks -
all the women love me,
they cuddle me for weeks.
Well, that's my little story,
that's all I have to tell -
I'm just a little angel -
welcome to Hell - ha, ha, ha.

Ken Price

THE LULL BEFORE THE STORM

*(A carefree cruise in the Gulf of Mexico off Florida,
September 7th through 11th, 2001)*

On seventh of September, in 0-1
We left Tierra Verde far behind
And sailed due south in early morning sun
Towards Captiva Island, where we'd find
South Seas Resort, that paradise on Earth.
How wonderful it was to get away;
Replace the rat race with five days of mirth,
Of carefree laughter, self-indulgence, way
Beyond the bounds we set ourselves at home.
And so we talked, we snacked, we drank, we swam,
We sunbathed, walked, we dined, we spa'd in foam.
We felt so free, we did not care a damn!
Yet on our journey home came news to fear,
That fight we must for all that we hold dear.

Christopher Head

CHARLIE IS M'DARLING

When we met I was only twenty-one.
You, sitting on the table, looked so fair,
I thought you looked enticing, might be fun,
with just that hint of danger in the air.

Next time we met I recognised your smile
and picked you up pretending to be brave.
I kept my distance for a little while,
then got together careful to behave.

So courtship started, our first kiss,
the rush of blood, the pounding heart,
I closed my eyes, in perfect bliss,
enraptured, captured, from the start.

But now I find you are imperious,
I do your bidding, eager for your call;
but your demands are far too serious,
with me disarmed, completely in your thrall.

Dementedly in love, it will be hard
for me to part and not touch you again.
Goodbye! Go mark another lover's card
my darling sweetheart, dearest love, cocaine.

Peter Huggins

WORDS OF ENCOURAGEMENT

One more big effort
When the chips are down.
Don't give up now,
Don't wear a frown.

Just steel yourself,
Have another go.
You may not win,
But put on a show.

Finish the course
You once desired.
Begin again,
Ambition fired.

One deep breath
Then start anew
And finish
What you set out to do.

The chips slipped down,
And the fish, with ease,
Now just do the same
With the mushy peas.

R L Cooper

A TWIST IN THE TALE

It was love at first sight
I remember the afternoon, the night
We met at a college friend's party
We were both hail and hearty.
She told me she worked on the bus
I accepted without question or fuss.
After all, it was in the vacation
Which filled us with and brought elation.
We danced and ate cake
And then it was time to go.
To say goodnight, goodbye, it was late.
I walked with her to the stop to catch her last bus
It had gone, once again no fuss.
Until she died it brought us and we were together
To face all kinds of weather
For she stayed with me that night
Which turned out and proved to be just right.

Allan John Mapstone

THE FIRING SQUAD

Mouth, dry as a desert
Heartbeat, fast, irregular
Palms sweating, vision blurred
Sounds in the head like high voltage pylons.

Moisture in scalp and on forehead
Weakness in knees and limbs
Stomach like a band of steel
Bowels in danger of spilling.

So what must he feel like
The man in the blindfold
Stood awaiting the bullet?
I am just one of the firing squad!

Edward A Walker

VISITORS FROM SPACE?

Down they came from silvery craft,
Men now cried, where once they'd laughed.
What would these invaders demand?
Few would dare ignore their command.

Long ago the Norsemen had come,
Viking axes made the air hum,
Remembering this we stood in fear,
What awful fate would we now hear?

Surprise and joy as this great host,
From Father, Son and Holy Ghost,
Their outer garb shed as in storm,
To reveal their angelic form!

D Spanton

WHAT'S ON

On the dot you open the doors
Leap smartly out of the way,
Or risk your life
Being trampled on
In the most alarming way.

You can't compare the rush hour
With this madly swarming lot,
A football crowd
Would stand and stare
In timid little knots.

It's not feeding time at the zoo
r a boy scout jamboree,
Or folk gone mad
At a boxing match,
When they don't like the referee.

They haven't come for sport, you see,
No rush for train or bus,
Oh no, it's just
A jumble sale,
That's causing all the fuss . . .

Joan Hammond

BEE-KEEPER

With smoke hands harvest
Caves of sticky summer gold
You dance with nature.

Brenda Dove

NATURE

Nature all loving we must obey
Rarely good for us to have our own way
From babe content to be at mother's breast
To old man being natural is best.

Nature we sometimes resent in our mood
We then find it has not been for our good
The sun, moon, stars never fail to appear
Spring, summer, autumn every year.

Water, the nectar of life, free for all
Sunshine to ripen before the fruits fall
Diseases and pests can be washed away
Farewell to bacteria cannot stay.

Men clone animals and try to change seed
Spurred on by competition and by greed
May find that their ideas come from hell
But if man follows nature all is well.

Peter Arthur Butcher

TOTAL ECLIPSE 1999

We drove through quietness
In Picardy.
Past fields of sunflowers
Hanging heavy heads
Appropriately.
We drove towards the park
An area of totality.
It was a cloudy day
We didn't expect to see
The eclipse in all its majesty
But with precision
At the appointed hour
The clouds dispersed.
There was a toenail sliver
Out of the sun.
It crept along
Carving its way to darkness
To total and sombre night.
For two minutes
It was as if the vast crowd
Held its breath
No sound, no movement
Then in the west
A startling dawn
And life returned
With a diamond in the sky.

Olga M Momcilovic

SEASONS AT THE RED MILL

Winter's mantle, and icy streams,
Waterwheel still, cold moonlight gleams.
The robin's eagle eye and ruddy breast,
Tells us all that nature is at rest.

Spring at the Red Mill and all is waking,
The waterwheel, starts shuddering and shaking.
Sending its froth and bubbles into the moving stream,
And the watery sun now sheds its beam.

Summer's here, with a sky of azure blue,
Yellow-throated daisies and butterflies new.
Magnolias and rhododendrons bloom,
All set to chase away winter's gloom.

Autumn creeps in, with mists and dew,
The trees lose their leaves of red and gold,
Rosehips and berries, show their colours bold,
The mill is peaceful now, as summer bids adieu.

Red Mill by the stream, waterwheel in flow,
A boat floating near and the riverbanks put on their show,
The trees are dressed in splendour, regal and serene,
The seasons fly past here, an ever-changing scene.

Anne Roberts

SECRET HOLLOW

Hidden leafless glade
discovered long ago
small gems, white faces sought
mid-winter quest to go
the joy of that same glade today
multiplied myriad tiny flowers
their beauty spread woodland carpets
flakes like snow-scattered frozen showers

in silent splendour
possessing secret hollow
enchantment promising warm days to follow
snowdrops perfect heralds dressed in white
sentinels in miniature
installed by nature's might

small, white faces once elusive
so difficult to find
innocent of power yet effectively
today most ruthless kind
great clusters invade spilling over pathways
transforming secret hollow in radiance
blooms descendant beyond belief
covering old haunts of play
mid-winter quest secret snowdrops
hidden memories yesterday.

Mildred F Barney

IN THE HEART OF THE HILLS

In the heart of the hills
stunned by magnificence,
a silence spreads.

In the soaring heights
with such wide flung views
words have no place.

In the heart of the hills
the silence speaks
as a buzzard mews
and an eagle barks.

From the glen below
a great stag roars,
and the waters churn
down the narrow gorge.

In the heart of the hills
alone in space
the mind expands
as wilderness calms.

Today in dreams
old limbs retrace
steps to the summit snows
in the heart of the hills.

Pam Russell

THE APPLE TREE

Apples falling
From the apple tree
If only you had wings
Felt the gentle breeze
Kiss you in the trees.

Helen Owen

WINTER'S FINGERS

Winter's fingers
Have started to grip the land
As the Nene Valley
Feels his icy grip
Autumn surrenders
In hedgerows of brown and gold
Below clear blue skies
Towers and monuments
Are visible below a smoky horizon
Gloved fingers grip
Steering wheels
Oblivious to winter's
Forthcoming beauty.

Paul Wilkins

OWL

Eyes which glow as day,
In hoot and gloaming thicket
Espy the scurried prey.

Sideways hitched,
Deep entranced,
Talons grip the crooked branch.

Sops the graveyard tombs,
Mistled puddles silver swing
Pewter mirror, mirror moons.

Fat grey rats are first away,
Lychgate cats leap to the fray.

Roger Mosedale

A Shell

A
Shell
Is
Little
And
Brittle
And
Small
Like
Baby's
Feet
Before
Old
Age.

Nicola Barnes

SEALIFE

Snails, shrimps and crabs galore,
Plenty to find and lots lots more.
Rocks, weed and mother of pearl,
Shells and limpets that really curl.

There are all kinds of fish in the sea,
Some you can catch and eat for tea.
Lots of colour there will be,
Blue's, yellow's and red's all three.

Turtles and terrapins are full of shell,
And some can have a really bad smell.
Some are big and some are small,
They are never, never tall.

A dolphin is a wonderful mammal,
It hasn't a hump so it isn't a camel.
It swims about in the sea,
Very gay and full of glee.

The sea lions swim and dive down deep,
They only have to have a peep.
After some fish for their tea,
As they move around the sea.

The walrus comes on to the land,
And porpoises are just grand.
Octopus and jellyfish really are not my dish,
All in all they are just not fish.

Whales could be the largest ones,
As they swim and show their tums.
Twenty, thirty feet or more,
That is more than just a score.

Penguins are another source,
They are black and white of course.
They walk on shore as well as swim,
The sea is full of wonder within.

Eileen Denham

THE CHURCH CLOCK OF ST JULIEN DES LANDES

Silent moon, welcoming in your warmth,
As you play hide-and-seek with us through the darkened trees,
A soothing tone as we return from late night showers to our maxi tent,
Hearing the owls' intimate cry amidst the silent domain of La Foret,
A soothing environment to march in time with one another,
Along with the alluring chimes of the clock of St Julien,
Striking midnight it resonates into our souls, sadly dimmed!
Yet in this rural isolation beyond even reason a silent
                                   harmony rests within,
To clear our sometimes muddled lives and restore perspective,
As the clock chimes I sense a village still living and
                                   bound in resistance France,
And then in mystery the bells repeat again 4 minutes later!
I wonder why?

Martin Norman

AN OBSERVATION

The wind blows the sycamores.
The leaves wave.
The rowan rustles less,
because of smaller branches.

Keith Murdoch

THE SEA

Soothing voice, reflections,
Sailing ships, watery grave,
Salt, seasickness, white lace,
Towering waves, powerful friend, enemy,
Corrosive force undermining cliffs,
Heroism Grace Darling.
Beauty of Northumberland coast,
Sand beach, tropical island,
Way of transferring coconuts to other
Islands,
Pirates, Neptune, Davy Jones,
Mermaids, frothy beer, dragon sea,
Sewerage, coldness, North sea,
Radiation, seaweed, sirens,
Crunching pebbles,
Toes disappearing into damp sand,
Surfing, wall of water,
The flood will it come again?
The poles melting,
Tow Law in the safe zone . . . is Crook?
Flood the Sahara . . . how long before
Usable land?
How many times has the Mediterranean
Dried out?
Collecting a shell necklace.
Swimming nude in the Mediterranean.
Green or blue. Ginger biscuits, Moon
Tides, turbulent, ominous, crashing,
Challenging, ships' graveyards,
Galleons, shipwrecks, underworld,
Shoals, sharks, blackness, coral,
Danger, constant motion, mirror-like.

Mary Armstrong

THE SWANS

An artist might with envy try
To capture this enchanting view,
But I am left with words alone
To portray my thoughts to you.

Beneath the bridge in Leamington,
The River Leam flows on and on,
And rushing waters from the weir
Obscure the sound of sweet bird-song.

Upon the banks on either side,
Graceful weeping willows grow -
Dip branches to the water's edge
And mask the river's endless flow.

Taking shelter in this sanctuary
A pair of perfect swans rest there,
And close to them two cygnets hide,
The loving family in their care.

Forward they glide, as close they dare,
And with tender eyes they plead
From the figures standing on the bridge
Somehow to help them feed.

Puts things in true perspective
In this busy life we lead;
These creatures ask so little
To help make their lives complete.

Joan Mathers

AUTUMN

The grey-clad morning breaks
And finds that sleepy autumn wakes.

Autumn - when leaded clouds
Weep fretful rain,
Beating on the windowpane,
Like tears confessing better days
When all reflected summer's rays.
Heed not the merciless tattoo,
But seek for autumn's rosier hue.

Though naughty winds blow leaves to sweep
Crunching and floating round our feet,
See orange, yellow, brown and red,
Leaves that are everywhere we tread,
Beautiful, but sad to see
The naked arms of every tree.
But note the berries shining bright,
Glistening in the weak sunlight,
Produce that is nature bred,
Orange, yellow, brown and red.

See the happy squirrels play,
Foraging throughout the day,
Gleaning up their nutty store,
Dropped from oak on forest floor.
Tho' the season wreaks of dying,
And the winds are softly sighing,
Raise your eyes and see the glory
Of the seasonal autumn story.

Then round the fire with dog do lie,
Forget sad autumn slipping by.

Aleene Hatchard

A Walk In The Rain

A walk in the rain
All alone with your thoughts
In the forest
At the top of the hill
Pine trees and birch
Rhododendrons and ferns
Bramble thistle and holly
To reminisce of the times you had had
The good times, the bad
The happy times, the sad
A walk in the rain
All alone with your thoughts
In the forest
At the top of the hill.

Greeny

AS WE SOAR - ENGLAND OUR ENGLAND

Through feathered clouds I proudly look
See your patterned quilt a glowing on the ground.
Intricately made, admired by all - this woven covering of fertile soil.
Your browns and greens make colourful patches.
Those shiny jewels are rows of houses, spiky turret erect and tall
And as the power of jet's ascending, quilted pattern's revealed to all.

More beds of fluffy feathers seem motionless, but still in flight we soar
Palest blue meets brightest white.
Is there break in ozone layer?
Are we riding on a wing and a prayer?
Down through clouds the shorelines seen.

Snow-covered plains but not a soul in sight.
What I fear maybe an imagery plight.
Rumpled tufts appear, could it be that children played there?
Snow's a-melting now, but is it really so - water can be seen, way below
Trickling streams are now a-forming, down the glades,
melted snow.

Lakes and streams are adjoining.
Snow's disappearing, like butter melting on fresh baked dough
Span of water's getting wider, I am 'wandering slowly as a cloud . . .'
Who is there to share this with me: tingle in the heart, this lovely glow.
Banks of snow are now appearing, who's been shovelling in the night?
Bright light, white light, day light, modern painting's in the sky
Of fluffy clouds that are too shy.

Look way down there, see cloth of sheerest voille
Further on see tulle with blobs of pointed cream.
Rough roads are coming up, bumps and dips are strongly felt
Turbulence is forecast, 'Fasten seatbelts!'
Fear in me I'm getting thirsty but not a hostess in sight.
We are gliding very smoothly, new roads are felt beneath the wheels.
Feet outstretched and I am comfy in this upgraded 'club' space.

A C Yap-Morris

THE WATERFALL

Up in the hills, far away
The water starts to flow.
Over the rocks it will tumble.
The speed of the water will grow.

Rushing past the grassy banks
And under the weeping trees.
As it flows swiftly downwards
The spray is caught by the breeze.

Watering all the bankside plants
Which grow so lush and green.
Washing all the pebbles and rocks
So they constantly have a sheen.

Then finally over the top it goes
Crashing to the rocks below.
As the sun shines on the watery spray
We see all the hues of a rainbow.

In the depth under the waterfall
Fish take great delight
In this beautiful clear water
Sparkling in the sunlight.

Lynne Walden

THE SOIL

A simple chore like digging gives delight,
Perhaps a centipede comes into sight,
Or else a juicy worm or spider red,
For soil is full of life and never dead.

Bacteria in their billions flourish here
To human sight unable to appear,
For much exists that we may never see
Yet, in its microscopic world is meant to be.

And as the gardener adds the rich manure
He seeks a richer harvest to secure;
The enriched creatures of the soil rejoices
Red robin on the spade has cheerful voice.

For, on the fertile soil we all depend;
It is for us its future to defend,
That we may live, and in good health to stand
Forever blest with bounty from the land.

Vere Collins

AUTUMN MOODS

Moody autumn swings from mellow
Sun-drenched days, red fruit and leaves,
Ripened cornfields, golden yellow,
To melancholy night that grieves
The passing of the summer heat,
A pall of mist enwraps the trees,
Sunless days of rain and sleet,
Falling leaves swirl on the breeze.

Morning sun is brittle bright,
Afternoon, a golden glow,
Gusty winds invade the night,
Scattering twigs and leaves below,
Daybreak dawns all misty damp,
Leaf-lorn branches hushed and still,
Sun appearing like a lamp,
Lights the dewdrops on the hill.

Sometimes autumn bids the summer
Such a lingering 'goodbye'
Borrowing mellow sunshine from her,
Colouring the leaves on high
In final glory 'ere they turn to brown,
All too soon the cold winds blow,
Damp leaves cling to frozen ground,
Winter time has said 'Hello!'

Ailsa Keen

CANAL MISTS

The mist that engulfs a canal evokes childhood dreams,
Dreams which long lay dormant waiting to be roused
For mist has a shroud-like quality that can frighten
Or a movement that defies control,
It reaches the depths of mind and etches on the soul.

What lies behind the cloak of white?
What shapes come looming nigh?
Do dragons live within this gloom
Or perhaps a monster with huge claws?
The thought can make the heart skip beats and pause.

But when the mist is slowly clearing
As if a hand was lifting it aside,
Shapes appear which are familiar and calm the dreams,
The terror goes and is replaced by security and peace
And our fears once more unfounded set to cease.

Gillian Ackers

ONLY THE GALLANT

The winter's turf frozen
Sceptic circles of mushrooms
Sporing seeds like dust clouds
Birds drinking almost like a
Barn owl kissing bye bye
To rodents for the squire.
Infested the riverbank laps
Away the gentle day.
As swans and geese make their
Way wading like golden wind
Chuckling ripples like the ones
On my back become content.
The HMS Victory stood in a dry
Dock whilst the maiden journey,
Splice the mainbrace and
Good wine and rum too.
The Albatross so willed
Strong and true makes me
Shiver me timbers
Save the Arctic blue.

Hardeep Singh-Leader

TIMELESS

From the bus
Saw a man
In the city park.
Homeless his tag,
The only one to have time,
Feeding the birds
From a brown paper bag.

Bernadette O'Reilly

THE SUNFLOWER

Head raised in golden glory
Face toward the sun
Stretching on such stately stems
Prepared for things to come

Petaled in rustic beauty
Sepal of richest black
Fruitful seeds provide so much
In cereal, oil and fat

Feathered friends feed greedily
From seeds amidst the soil
Graceful head bowing sadly
Tattered skirt now spoilt

With bronzed tips now faded
All riches have been taken
Your bounty is now graded
Your husk is now forsaken

You stood once in your beauty
The gifts you gave we'll treasure
You have performed your duty
Created so much pleasure

Oh, you golden glory
Once faced toward the sun
Completed is our story
Now your work is done.

Linda Mary Hodgson

UNTITLED

If you stand close to a tree
At the end of summer
And listen -
You will hear the leaves
Dropping one by one -
Caught by the wind
Floating to the ground
And blowing down the street.
Summer is finished -
In spring,
The leaves will come again,
A re-birth of beauty -
To brighten all our lives
And you can stand
Close to the tree
And listen . . .

Jean Chartres

WINTER GLORY

Dark December nights constrict the mornings
Squeezing snowflakes from a gasping sky
Frozen souls grip, jagged, to the starlight
Where dreams of summer loving scamper by

Wrapped in pure white blankets, earth lies sleeping
Though frosty fingers prod the days awake
Time but tiptoes by, the hours creeping
As fragile, brittle dawns appear and break

Exploding on the scene a north wind plunders
The silence of this hypothermic cloud
Here settled over each and every life form
Now battered by a voice pitched way too loud

Winter, harsh and raging in her glory
Refusing to be meek and soon dismissed
Casts an icy shadow on the landscape
And lowers one almighty, angry fist.

Kim Montia

The Red May Rose

I wandered through the woods today
And heard the lapwing cry.
It was the early days of May,
The earth was warm and dry.

I came across a clearing there,
With a brook that gently flows
And saw a sight so sweet and rare,
An early red May rose.

In grandeur there it stood amidst
Trees tipped with verdure green,
Slightly shrouded in the mist,
A delightful woodland scene.

A crimson splash in wooded glade,
By the brook the rose bush grows,
Lack lustre tints and other shades
Bedraggled by the rose.

It nods and bows its scarlet head
In the gentle evening breeze,
Roots deep below its woodland bed,
A red feast for honeybees.

In future days and years ahead,
Before life comes to a close,
I'll see again that mossy bed
Of that early red May rose.

Denis O'Doherty

AN AUTUMN DAY

Seven o'clock in the morning
and my cycling day has begun.
The sun shines in a turquoise sky,
through fluffy, grey-white clouds,
giving them a gilded edge.
A flock of gulls flies overhead,
their white plumage glinting star-like,
as they wheel around enjoying flight.
Straight lines of young green barley
form artistic, gently curving lines
with the rise and fall of the land.
Autumn is here - enjoy it all!

Patricia Anne Ray

THE MESSENGER

It floated gently on the breeze;
O'er grasses green and leafy trees,
A silver globe in gentle flight;
Caressed by nature's rosy light:
A messenger whose edifice was formed;
Its entity and shape adorned
To spiral upwards from the ground;
Ride the wind and settle down:
Perhaps upon a hidden track;
Concealed within some nook or crack:
To rest a torpid, drowsy ball;
Till Mother Nature fained to call:
And then with potency imbued;
A fresh awakening is infused:
Seeds may fade, but some will last;
Defy cold winter's icy blast;
Weather, sunshine, wind and rain;
Be masters of their own domain.

Alexander Hamilton

FINGERPRINTS LEFT IN EDEN

The morning rises with you
Sharp sunlight in dewy grass
Shines bright like bladed glass
Under the careful tread of your bare feet
Though I know the map of your bones
You have left nothing in my bed
Only remembrances -
It is never enough
I long to touch the light
That is your light
I long to rise and follow . . .
But you are gone.
Through the arms of the apple trees
You sweep like a dancer silently
And your silence cuts
Through the shadows
Like a song
While I,
My dreams broken spill
From torn sleep
Like red rock out of a fissure
Falling, falling, falling
With nothing to hold on to.
Let me tell you
I want to be the tree
You throw yourself around
And hug so tight
Its light is crushed in your arms.
It's not for nothing I call you Eve,
Hands clasped to the bark
In the first light
Of aching desire.

Afterwards I will find it
And discover
Your touch
Fingerprints left in Eden
I swear I will never forget you!
How could I?

Tom Quinn

A MOMENT OF MEDITATION

From where does this come?
And stretches out of its rays on us, some
Birds take their instruments and sing,
Flowers and trees on their rhythm swing,
Animals join in with groans and cries
Greeting that sun that began to rise.
Their song reaches the hunter's ear
Who took his gun and by their death he swears.
But as their way is now clear
Nothing, yes, nothing can cause their fear.

Boudarouafi Abdelrhani

SPRING

O brave little hyacinths and windswept daffodils,
Nestling primroses in clusters o'er the hills,
Pussy willows, catkins reign supreme
All along the banks of many a rippling stream.

Violets, even cowslips, join this merry throng,
Cherry blossom sheds its shower of petals all the way along,
I never cease to wonder how there are so many
And how God made them all without a single penny.

A Hankey

RAIN

The clouds hover darkly.
The wind creeps through cracks.
We stare through rain-drenched windows
At the hidden sky
Or walk, eyes down,
Water gurgling around damp feet.

But look suddenly with a
Level gaze, rain trickling
Over you and see
The trees, the grass,
Dazzle with green.
The whole earth is dipped
And dipped in vats
Of emerald dye,
While yet more drips and
Runs to fill the aching
Streams.

Trees flap damply in the wind
Like sheets, like sails.
Daffodils lie flat and shine
On the grass,
Yellow beyond belief.
Fallen blossom surrounds them,
Pink and white among daisies
Shut tight and waiting.

Spring has almost gone.
Washed to a perfect
Pitch of greenness.
Gone while we watched
The sky, waiting for
The wind to change.

A L Skevington

EAGLE VIEW

I stand
On the edge of creation.
My feet grip rock
Bared by wind and rain;
Vertebrae of the mountain.

Beneath,
Valleys
Brown and green;
Villages, terracotta and white,
Shimmer in the heat.

Beyond,
Pale skies in deepening blues;
Far-off hills;
Distant peaks.

Above,
Ravens swooping and cawing
Among craggy ledges
That crowd beneath the sky
While, on silent wing,
An eagle soars
Into the sunlight.

A J Roberts

CELTIC HEARTBEAT

Fast moving great, grey duster clouds
Harshly polish an already well-scrubbed sky
And sigh.
A slogan-streaked delivery van
Reading *Pride Of The Clyde*
Throwing up fine spray on the cold, wet motorway.
Curls of sheep dotting soft, damp hillsides
Straying far from grey stone farms.
Cows confined in lush, milky pastures
By jigsawed, dry stone dykes.
Pheasants by the roadside stroll
Mists on heather, languid roll
Clouds unfurl, draw shafts of light.
Moon is chased by wind and weather.
Velvetly caresses heather.
Skies, like nowhere else can form - slip from grandiose to storm.
And weary kestrels call forlorn
Into the city's orange, sodium night.
Ghostly forms all cast around
On the breathing, steamy ground
Making not the slightest sound.

Marilyn Hodgson

BEAUTY

There's beauty all around us
for everyone to see.
A beauty fit for a king
and even folk like you and me.

The colours of the rainbow.
The hue of autumn leaves.
The sparkling white of winter snow
and the gold of harvest sheaves.

All these and falling rain,
the warmth of summer sun,
are a special gift, given to us.
To each and every one.

Julie Brown

THIS IS A SPECIAL MOMENT IN TIME

Leaves floating through the autumn air,
Floating from an old oak here and there,
Lying on the path ahead,
Spreading everywhere.

Great branches soon are bare
And autumn song is in the air,
Like a symphony in the night
Extending into morning light.

I like to probe the mystery of life,
Autumn, colour and beauty
I am filled with this morning glory
With birds gliding with the river tide.

Milly Saunders Farren

MY VIEW

I took my picnic with me and sat beside the stream
While I pondered on the miracle of life,
I marvelled at the mystery of the dancing dragonflies
As they lived a lifetime in a single day.

Beyond the sparkling water on the sun-drenched hazy hills
Little lambs cavorted in their play;
Living every moment as though it were their last
And never mind the passing of their days.

A field of waving corn adorned the bank across the river
Vying with the movement of the stream
And scarlet poppies dazzled the field mice pilfering grain
And I wondered if life were but a dream.

And as I gazed in silent wonder at the azure sky above me.
At the hills, lambs, pasture land and river
I knew my body, mind and soul completed the whole
Of God's eternal miracle of life.

Beryl Wicker

WIRRAL SUNSET

How I wish I had the talent,
To paint this breathtaking sight,
The sun setting behind Hilbre Island,
The drawing nigh of night.

Around me the shadows are lengthening,
An awesome sight to behold,
The sun reflected in waters below,
A rippling pathway of gold.

I will always remember this dying ember,
The sun is sinking fast,
Mesmerised by the reddening sky,
I watch it to the last.

The Wirral sunset, I will never forget,
I feel rather sad, quite forlorn,
The sun is now gone - I cheer at the thought,
Our loss is another man's dawn.

Jean Burch

THE FOUR SEASONS

Winter - so dark and dismal
Until it starts to snow
Then we awaken up to wonderland
And get lifted out of woe

Spring - so fresh but sometimes keen -
Time for a really good spring clean
Bulbs are sprouting in the ground
Colour will soon be all around

Summer - the time to relax in the sun
Get the sun beds out and have some fun
Barbecues smoking, gardens full of flowers
We might even welcome some well-timed showers!

Autumn and the Fall - the most beautiful time of all
Reds and gold abound with the leaves upon the ground
It's sad that summer has passed us by
But now, I'm afraid, we're winter-bound

Isn't nature wonderful?
In a mere twelve months so beautiful?
Different seasons - different colours
And just to think - *they are all ours!*

Patricia Holloway

THE GOOD THINGS IN LIFE

A smile when things go wrong
to help the day along;
My mother's gentle voice
to guide my every choice.

My cats curled by the fire
home comforts they desire;
My dogs to welcome me
with unaffected glee.

A favourite book to read
fulfils escapist need;
A tranquil solitude
inclines to thoughtful mood.

A sunrise o'er the hills
with pleasure my heart fills;
A robin pecking crumbs -
each winter morn he comes.

The quiet of a wood
with rowan trees in bud;
First snowdrops brave the cold -
to heaven their leaves unfold.

A pheasant's wondrous feathers;
the moors bedecked with heathers.
A buzzard's eerie cry;
wild geese across the sky.

So when you're feeling sad -
consider good not bad;
Reflect on Nature's way -
be thankful for each day.

Mary Farrell

As Evening Falls

The hedgehog wakes and sniffs the air
as the evening draws nigh.
Round the pond and across the lawn
he shuffles with a sigh.
This little creature stops and peers,
as he reaches the chestnut trees
and just beyond the moonlit garden
the thatched cottage appears.

He licks his lips and shuffles on
at the very thought of food
and the lady who waits for him
is so reliable too.
The silver moon grins as he lights up
the evening sky
and looks down upon the ghostly garden
as the hedgehog shuffles by.

Pauline Potts

AT DAWN OF DAY

Now if you close your eyes
You'll miss the wonderful dawn
And all the marvellous things
To be seen on a bright, sunny morn.

The dew on the grass,
Spiders' webs that glisten,
Trees bathed in dawn light
And so too you must listen.

Don't shut your ears
For you'll hear the first birdsong
In a wonderful chorus
Sending up to God their prayers.

So walk in the long grass,
Hold your head up high
Then perhaps you will see
A multicoloured butterfly

With its gossamer wings
Flitting up high to find the light
Skimming among the little things
Weaving and dancing with delight.

In quietness commune with the Lord
Gaining strength for the day
Thank Him for the little things
Then try to walk His way.

Eunice Squire

Spring To Life

I will look out now
And see my garden bright.
Bright as a spring morning,
But in an evening light.
An evening night so tender
And damp as a morning dew.
The dampness of those raindrops
Make everything anew
And I can see that evening light
Fading fast away,
Away to another tomorrow
And another perfect day.

Pat Maddalena

NATURE IN ART

Without the presence of the Malvern Hills
I would never have been inspired to write,
On solitary walks it's the heart that fills,
Stirred by such wondrous beauty to the sight.

Approaching the hills soon enter a trance
Thoughts borne on the wind caressing my face,
Rhythms in my head make me want to dance,
With arms outstretched lifting in an embrace.

The Malvern Hills rising sheer, compelling,
More majestic, somehow, when bathed by sun,
Where souls meet nature, their secrets telling,
That moment, becoming one, all is won.

The Malvern Hills, alluring, sensual,
Sometimes sublime, deeply spiritual.

Betty Mealand

TILL THE END OF TIME

Words can never make me feel,
The wonder that I see,
Looking out onto the ocean blue,
The waves are calling me,
Showing me the power of life,
Telling me to be strong,
Open my mind to nature's way,
Hear the wind singing our song.

No matter what the future holds,
The ocean will show the way,
Giving us a reason to go on,
How to live our lives each day,
No matter how hard a storm breaks,
Or how peaceful a day may be,
The ocean is there to show us,
We are here for eternity.

When you are trapped in the city
And your days are all filled with pain,
Think of the sound of the ocean,
Walk out in the pouring rain,
The wind will bring you nature's song,
Hear the words bringing peace to you,
Telling you that you will be free,
To be part of the ocean so blue.

Lesley Allen

TREES

We grow together in the cool, green forest
enjoying nature's gifts of sun, wind and rain.
My girth expands year after year
making me look strong and fearless.
Sometimes though, I envy the slim pine
caring for her young saplings.
Weeping willow beside us possesses much beauty
but yet so sad as she bends, trailing her foliage
to the river's edge.
Rarely looks up or smiles.
Silver birch contrasts, standing tall and elegant
waving branches at the passer-by.
As evening shadows cover, I creak and groan with years.
But all around are rustlings and whisperings
As we slumber together on the forest bed.

Hazel Wilson

SWAN SOUND

A flight of swans, heraldic fly
    above the sea.
Their wings the colour of the sky,
    plumed rocketry.
White-winging sings in my ears,
    ringing to pierce my mood,
    moved at their beauty.
The leader whistles and curving,
    veers inland;
Leaving me standing alone
    to carry,
    in my mind, a sound force
    vibrating through all my time.

The flight of nine, in line, save two
    coupled to one side.
Initialling in space your name,
    holding you, cloud-bound;
And I,
    to marvel at your claim on me.

Janine Vallor

PWLLHELI

The harvest moon was shining
Above the mountains high!
Many a falling star fell out the deep blue sky
As I stood gazing into the enchanting night!
If only you had been there to share it with me
The scene I have just described
Of one night in Pwllheli!

Rosina Jarman (Nee Grist)

NIGHT ON THE NILE

Anchored, tied up to large boulders,
we settled on board for the night.
In the wet darkness birds flapped among
the reed beds, disturbing the calm.
Just then, the moon, as if switched on
in the sudden darkness of sundown,
lit up the withered deck outside the cabin door.
Its beam played among the ropes and rails
as we gently swayed.
It was difficult to turn in for the night,
more pleasant on deck in the balmy air.
Once inside, out we go again,
just one more glance.
The frosted orb is hoisted now between two palms,
Its nocturnal throne bleached white with light.
Who could sleep in the presence of such a sight?

Mavis Abernethy

Yesterday, Today, Tomorrow

The clock is ticking and the sun is shining,
The day is new and night seems a long way away,
A gentle breeze brushes across the grass and trees,
Blowing around in every way.

The birds are singing upon their perch,
Trying to hide in the shade,
From the heat of the sun,
Hoping for the sun to fade.

In the distance the moon appears,
And night is drawing near,
The sun goes until tomorrow,
The singing birds are silenced until morning
When we can listen to their cheer.

Kimberly Harries

WET

Pendle Water rambling over the rocks
autumn leaves dive
ducks swim fast
river
gone.

Robert Shooter

THE LANDSCAPE

For England's heart is singing
Amongst the trees, with gentle breeze
Only leaves' sweet charms,
Overlooking the midland glen.

Time! What is time
Which treasures the memory,
Through the realm of England's story
And the days of long ago.

Looking over the landscape
With a breath of the midland air
Passing of the days;
Time should borrow from the future,
                              to the present day.

Heather Aspinall

ETHEREAL BEAUTY

Stars shine so brightly in the night
twinkling, bringing much delight.
Ethereal brilliance for all to see
sparkling there, such rich beauty.

Heavenly splendour there to please
in the twilight ne'er to cease.
Such wonderment glistens on high
jewels to treasure in the sky.

So wish you now upon a star,
dreams and hopes to travel far.
Eternal glory glow away
such love within our heart to stay.

Margaret Jackson

LITTLE SPIDER

This web you weave is beautiful
With frost and dew upon the silk
Make pictures that give pleasure still
When sunlight catches every strand
Turns your web into spun gold
This little spider's web of silk

Spider, spider, spinning web
Making steps to your lair
One by one you do climb
To wait for guests to arrive
With open arms you greet them in
Then you gobble them with glee

Little spider, spinning silk
How could something so small
Spin this perfect web?
Every strand is so precise
As if you took a measure out
You're far too small to have a brain

I write in praise of little spider
Spinning silk from morn to night
You really have a lot to do
No wonder all your legs are long
They let you run away from me

I sit in wonder at your skill
To spin that perfect web
In the garden, is your home
Please, don't come in here
You frighten me, my home is spider free
Little spider stay out there, please.

Carole A Cleverdon

THE COMMON

At environs of town
the common supplicates,
in green and gold beseeches;
God's mightiness sweeps down
in quietude on reaches far
where hearts and minds still peaceful are.

Grandeur of oaks surrounds
the grasses, dignifies
each moist resilient blade,
charisma stress impounds;
here heavy burdens are made light
dissolved in spaciousness and height;

mountain ash glints in sun,
jingles its silver grey
rediscovered jewellery,
a way of wonder won
by nature on frippery bent,
laughing where subtle breezes went

and liberated cur,
exultant, varied breeds
frantic with delight cavort,
their black and tawny fur
imagination's self-taught sketch
on future, thoughtfulness much etch.

Ruth Daviat

NOVEMBER THE ELEVENTH

Reddish beeches, tall.
November amber leaves,
Look magnificent as they fall.
Shedding themselves from the trees.
Each falling leaf, a tender thought
Of remembrance, of loved ones, never again see.
Minute silence, millions of heartaches.
Long way from their land of their birth.
In foreign fields, their God chosen acres.
Golden, amber, yellow looking trees.
Falling; falling leaves.

B G Clarke

SNOWDROPS

The snowdrops bloom - and yet I know
    That born of wind and rain,
These flowers - so like the driven snow -
    Are part of joy and pain.

For joy and pain have each a part,
    Within our lives to play.
And smiles and tears come to the heart
    Most ever passing day.

And, if perchance the pain should be
    Almost too much to bear.
May some sad heart, within my life,
    Find snowdrops growing there.

Sharon Ellis

CLOUDS

Clouds scudding across the sky
In many shapes as they float by
Faces, birds, dragons, boat
Imagine them all as on they float
Making daisy chain below
Under clouds as white as snow
Soon take on an orange glow
Yellow, gold then fiery red
Tells all nature, time for bed.

Sonia Riggs

AUTUMN BOUGHS

High up in the oak-wood canopy
Autumn boughs begin to shed their leaves
In showers of golden rain, while down below
The forest floor shines crimson. Rainbow hues,
Sun-blent, combine with hidden fountain springs
To deck cold morning dew with diamond fire
As wisps of shimmering spray, as fine as film,
Arise from singing brooks. A greater swell
Soon comes upon the air as distant rivers,
Fed by autumn rains, now serenade
In labyrinthine wonder. Autumn boughs,
Mirrored in a dance of crystal streams,
Droop down toward those frothing, foaming rapids
'Midst oaken glades and lawns of emerald green.

Deep in the heart of Autumn's golden woods
A lonely murmur, achingly divine,
Arises like the purest melody -
Sweet harmony, though from Heaven above.
Its source, a fountain of spring with fine cascades,
Mineral-rich, wells up from nutrient earth
And mounts a moss-grown knoll, to plunge headlong
Through woodland shades of deepest green. And now
A thousand voices swell in unison
As nymphs and naiads dance upon the foam
Of curtained cataracts and roaring falls;
And autumn boughs, alive with crystal streams
Of heady and invigorating sap,
Join with Nature's splendour, soon to wane.

Robert D Hayward

BODMIN MOOR

We looked forward to spending most of the day out on the moor
To a stranger it may seem deserted, but knowing the lore
We found hidden flowers growing underfoot covered in dew,
Gathered and ate sorrel leaves and juicy whortleberries too.
Golden plovers wheeled overhead and kept an eye on their nest
But rabbits played and scuttling around we enjoyed the best.

With twigs on a flat stone we made a fire 'neath a shady tree
Filled up a tin kettle from a stream to make a pot of tea.
Wild cress grew in the clear water, we put it between our bread.
In the autumn sun, with bare feet, lay on our backs and read.
To remember such safe freedom as children aged twelve and eight
Will be unknown for youngsters today, parents would fear their fate.

Mary Beale

THE WIND

I love the wind.
It blows my fears away,
Makes secrets clear to me;
With all its strength,
It talks unceasingly,
In many tones,
Is master over all,
Where'ver it blows;
No one commands it
Forever free,
And from a Heavenly source,
Eternally.

Mary Hughes

I WONDER AS I WANDER

As I walked a stretch of the South Downs Way
I hoped to absorb and deeply ingest
The beauties of nature's magic carpet
Outspread around, but all my hopes were dashed:
A painful bout of grave self-questioning
Demolished any chance of simple enjoyment.
Insistent challenge struck at heart and head
Demanding to know the how, the why and the whence;
What role had humans played? Was there indeed
A higher cause, a first and final cause
Underlying, overseeing, summing
The myriad multicoloured jigsaw bits
Together depicting the pattern of being?

Torn by distracting doubts, I found myself
Approaching a level vale, a village
At its heart, precious gem in priceless setting.
Now I was all awake, aware, involved,
Allowing every curvilinear line
To work its will. Curvilinear indeed,
For smoothly rounded contours all about me
Made me feel there must have been a law
Against all angles, points and peaks; as if
Each hedge and shrub and tree had to be
Rounded off by experts skilled in topiary.

But then I saw the church, majestic steeple
Heavenward soaring, stabbing and transfixing,
Impaling, with the placid vale cosily
Cocooned and buxomly bosomed below.

Now there, I felt, if only I could work it out,
Is the cryptic answer to every doubt.

William Braide

THE FOX

On a dark moonless night
the air is still and eerily quiet.
Suddenly out of the darkness
a fox appears from nowhere.
Without a sound it stealthily crosses the road,
only stopping briefly to glance round
as it hears a car approaching.
For a moment dazed by the car's headlights,
its eyes are illuminated like sparkling diamonds
against the inky black sky.
Undaunted the fox continues on its way,
disappearing through the hedge
and into the night just as suddenly as it appeared.

Karen Tilson

DAWN

How beautiful to behold, the arrival of dawn,
when all is hushed, with the passing of night,
where clouds unfurl their infinite beauty to greet the morn,
and the rising sun in all her glory, throws forth her wondrous light.

Lacy spiders' webs shrouded in a misty dew,
blow softly against the early morning breeze,
and the tiniest flowers awaken from their sleep,
where giant trees unfold their branches with gentle ease,
and the endless continuity of birdsong is ours to keep.

Another dawn, another dusk, another day, with
the solitude of fields of green, of endless
little streams, that flow on and on,
where butterflies are seen, gently at play,
how the warmth and elation, thoughts of your smile to me brings.

And how precious to my heart, are all of these special things.

Christine J Routledge

WINTER WONDERLAND

A magical feeling I have, when I see
The snow, like a blanket, all spread;
When silence has fallen, and all sounds are hushed,
As if life itself hangs by a thread!
Then, when the night falls and lamplights are lit,
The golden light shines over all;
The aura around holds one spellbound
Knowing not what may befall.

It seems time stands still and ev'rything's ceased,
Bating its breath - waiting for
Something wondrous to happen, or be released
To arrive and beguile us once more!
Will it be the White Queen, dazzlingly fair
Enthroned in her carriage so light,
Sparkling diamonds of ice encircling her hair,
As, with gauzy-winged fays, she takes flight?

No, it's not the Snow Queen; she's already been,
And ev'rywhere's still as before;
It's jolly Jack Frost round the corner I've seen,
With his ice bucket scattering more!
But we'll wait for the night-time again, now,
Praying with hearts full of hope,
That more snow will fall, blanketing all,
And we will be able to cope
With that marvellous, magical feeling that comes
When ev'rywhere's hushed all around
And, in wonderment stand and absorb it
As, yet again, it holds us spellbound.

Bee Wickens

SUMMER GLORY

Crescent winged bird gliding upon high,
Mobile sculpture, this, your domain;
The clear blue sky.

To a warm and gentle breeze you cling
But retain it you cannot, no matter how
- You try.

Let the atom, a button pressed, let nothing
- This marvel destroy.

The cuckoo's call drifts and fades
O'er greens of many shades.

The buttercups tall and the daisy bold,
Flowers of the wayside, see them unfold.

So much like the stories of old;
That garden of long ago.

Treasure the season and all its glory,
Hold onto the memory, and let it drift slow.

Clive Cornwall

ENGLAND'S TREASURE TROVE - SPRING

We went out driving with all the rest,
To see our countryside at its best.
We drove through countryside so green,
Spring is the best time for this scene.

In the late spring air a breeze did blow,
The clouds were hanging very low.
They soon dispersed and to our glee,
The sun through the clouds we began to see.

Green trees and many, many tubs,
A vast abundance of colourful shrubs.
The village gardens as we passed,
Were full of colour, blooms amassed.

Then through the lanes we then would go,
The fresh green leaves of the trees on show.
The oaks, the hawthorn, poplar and pine,
Along the verges they did line.

In churchyards and manor houses grew
Very many ancient yew.
The horse chestnuts were a lovely sight,
Masses of flower in pink and white.
We saw hawthorn bushes, that are called May,
It turned out to be such a lovely day.

We walked in the breeze, it was so fresh,
We felt the warmth of the sun on our new spring dress.
Then on our weary way we drove,
Through England's wonderful treasure trove.

Barbara Stanczyszyn

THE NORFOLK COAST

Strange, enchanting landscape,
that inspires a dormant imagination.
I sit alone on your sands,
in silent contemplation.

Watching the salty waters,
kiss the sunburnt sands.
Here there is time to appreciate,
the work of heavenly hands.

Behind me tower sad dunes,
that bare floral life galore.
The result of years of natural power,
as the sea carries the sand to shore.

Pebbles dash the golden sand,
washed up by the waves.
Dead crabs litter the water's edge,
rotting in open graves.

Looking out across the water,
to where the sea meets the sky.
A fishing boat lays far away,
nets hung out to dry.

My mind takes in this picture,
ready to be recalled again.
On a winter's night in London,
where it always seems to rain.

M A Challis

WINTER

Cold, dark nights and dismal days,
No bright skies, just blacks and greys,
Rain and wind, threatening cloud,
Thunderstorms, frightening and loud,
Barren trees, no blooming flowers,
Naked hedgerow, drowning showers.

Absence of birds, no morning song,
No more butterflies, gone so long,
Empty streets, deserted parks,
Children sad, no games or larks,
Wrap up well or catch a chill,
It will not last long, just until . . .

S M Hooper

MISTER HEDGEHOG

As I waddle along the street,
The autumn leaves fall at my feet,
I hate the cold, the frost and snow,
My face feels cold, my nose is red,
On days like this I'd rather be in bed,
My fleas are hopping mad with me,
I can't find a place to live, you see.
Will some kind person take me in,
I want to warm my toes,
What I really need is to be tucked up warm indoors,
I won't be any trouble, or leave my fleas with you,
I'll hibernate I promise, and sleep the winter through,
I'll wake when spring arrives again,
And the sun starts peeping through,
Being a hedgehog is not so bad,
And sleeping the winter through,
Is really what I am meant to do,
But through the winter bold this thought,
I will depend on you.

Terri Brant

A Winter's Tale

The snow has fallen.
Little robin redbreast
and the wild birds have come to visit,
leaving their stick-like prints in the snow.
The ice hangs from the trees,
the holly trees heavy with berries,
a scarlet red as if time had stood still
in a beautiful picture.
An artist's dream.
A Christmas theme.

Sylvia Morrow

SNOW

The snow looks bright
this Christmas day,
it came last night
from far away.
It danced in the air
then fell in the lane,
it covered the house tops
then danced again.
When all the world
was fast asleep,
the snowflakes fell
so white and deep.
What pretty shapes
come drifting down,
they sat on the church
without a sound.

Tom Clarke

THE MIST

Quietly the land receding, fading where the mist arose,
gradually his cold, grey breathing dampening the children's clothes.
Time of shadows, time of ghosts,
overall the mist comes close.
Unbeknown that he's near, suddenly a man appears,
Earthbound, muffled, deadly calm, causes confusion and alarm.
No more landmarks to display,
travellers they lose their way.
Dangerous, sinister is he,
spreads his cloak into the sea.
Hidden death arousing fear,
Bringing back, lost spirits here.
Hope for sun with one accord,
compelling man to stop and pause.
Long for his face, to glisten through,
give us back the earth we knew.
Shine like magic, mist is gone,
make man happy, child play on.
Disappeared into the air,
back inside his ghostly lair.
Autumn lover of the grey,
friends with the Reaper, night and day.

A E Doney

THE SUNSET

I never really noticed the beauty of the evening sky before,
During the winter walks I normally daydreamed
With my head down looking at the ground I walked on.
Although I have seen the ashen clouds before,
I never realised the splendour of their shapes
Until that one moment in time.
While walking one evening
I looked up at the sky and saw the sun setting
From the bright orange sky
And I sighed with amazement.
I watched the sun fall slowly to the earth,
In total silence, separated from the everyday life below
And then the trees lit up and dazzled,
Radiating with the beauty of the sun
And the world stood still as the clouds darkened
And the world entered night again
With a new witness
To its magic.

Agata Cibinska

TRANQUILLITY

Against the clamour of the world
I keep a quiet place.
No discord reaches to disturb
The calm bower where I trace
Life's path, and cull from its byways
Tranquil, changeless things, from which sweet comfort springs,
That will remain for future days.

My mother's smile, that through the years
Comes lovingly to me;
A golden pathway to the west.
At sunset, on the sea;
The plash of foam-topped breakers, toss'd
On shell-strewn sands, eternally; trees' winter tracery,
The dark earth glittering in the frost.

Shy violets found in early spring,
Half hid beneath wet leaves;
A well-loved tune that in the mind
A cheerful pattern weaves;
The silky fluff of a baby's hair
That brushed against my face; dew-spangled, glistening lace
Of cobwebs hanging in the morning air.

Thoughts such as these, of sights and sounds,
In memory's recess,
Lie tranquilly, until evoked
Some troubled mood to bless;
Their quiet joy the sad heart fills,
Life's frenzied rush is stilled, the mind with peace is filled,
Such bliss as Wordsworth found in daffodils.

Muriel Willa

THE FIRST . . .

Spring.
The first glimpse of the golden sun,
peeping out from the fluffy clouds.
The first birds cheerfully singing,
on a crisp, fresh, glistening morning.
The first glowing daffodil,
slowly creeping out of the soil, a law unto itself.

Summer.
The first kind smile,
from a person you once knew.
The first peaceful walk,
in the enticing woodland of the mountains.
The first chilling ice cream,
drips into the new open-toe sandals.

Autumn.
The first auburn leaves,
glide on the gentle, breeze.
The first flowers,
slowly fade into nothingness.
The first thundery skies,
hover above, waiting for a moment to make their presence known.

Winter.
The first delicate snowdrop,
floating down from the heavens above.
The first tingling chill,
creeping up the spines of shadowy figures.
The first smouldering smell,
haunts entangles the woodburning fire.

Grace Sutcliffe (17)

SUMMER REFLECTIONS

It was on the right day
And at the right time
In the warmth of summer
That we sauntered into this joyous place
This woodland walk
No need to talk
Our senses heightened with every step
A glimpse of blue through bursting green
To tease us through the undergrowth
And to the water's edge.

It was on the right day
And at the right time
In the heat of summer
That we indulged our eyes upon the lake
The sheer beauty to absorb
Of fragile dragonflies flitting everywhere
Ducks and ducklings circling reeds
Moorhens dancing on the lily pads
The white flowers cupped open to the sky
In the water's depth.

It was on the right day
And at the right time
In the height of summer
That we were startled by the brilliance
Of a perfect reflection
A boat house, mirror imaged in the water
Symmetrical in every way
In the sparkling clear ripples
A wondrous picture to recall - we stood
Enchanted at the water's edge.

Mair Walters

THE ROSE GARDEN

I walked into the rose garden,
and inhaled the perfumed flowers,
I suddenly felt a kind of peace,
and sensed its healing powers.
I thought this is God's creation,
He gave us the beauty of this,
to tread the paths in this special lace,
was sheer and utter bliss.
For weeks I'd been feeling quite depressed,
despondent and very low,
everything has seemed so wrong,
I didn't know which way to go.
As well as this, there was the war,
and the feelings it provokes,
not only on the ones who sin,
but all those innocent folks.
But now I know what I've to do,
I've to fold my hands and pray,
that God will do the best He can,
to lighten up my day!
For faith will move the mountains,
or this is what it's said,
please give me the strength to cope,
with whatever lies ahead.

Edith Antrobus

THE DANCERS IN CONTINUITY

The beech trees raise their palms to the skies
like Indian dancers posturing for pleasure or effect,
their russet robes cast carelessly aside upon the forest floor.
For this is autumn.

Soon their sinewy limbs will move no more,
stultified by the winter frost and snow.
A sombre stillness will descend on silent statues.
Spirits lie dormant.

They will dance again in spring, renewing their eternal vows,
although the music will have changed,
limbs moving tentatively, slowly coming back to life,
clothed shyly in diaphanous green, trembling in the light.
The timeless dance goes on.

Angela R Davies

THE GENTLE HAND OF NATURE

Early one morning, with the dew still fresh on the ground,
I happened upon a spider's web, newly spun,
Glistening in the weak rays of the rising sun.
I stood and stared. I moved closer and admired
Such diligence and workmanship, such fragile beauty
                                        and impressive span,
Only attainable by nature and chance, never replicable by man.

I see beauty in a spider's web.
I see beauty in rainbows and geese on the wing, moving noisily along.
And in wide-ranging oceans and skies bright with stars
And birds with their throats full of song.

Do you see such things? Or are you as blind as the rambling majority?
I would show you a world full of beauty if you would only be my love.
Let me show you through my eyes all the beautiful things I have seen.
Let me take you with my mind to every wonderful place I've ever been.

But would you be moved with appreciation for the glory of nature?
If your eyes do not see by themselves, if you feel no stirring
                                        in your mind,
No education from me can change it, you will always be blind.

I am not sorry for me that I cannot share my inner-self with you,
I am sorry for you and for all others who go through life
                with their eyes closed and their minds frozen.

When nature throws me a golden moment, I am glad to be there alone,
Feeling honoured and chosen. A delicate gift, given to one
                who will reward it with gratitude and memory.
Thus nature lays her gentle hand upon my swollen heart,
                for she knows that only loving eyes can see.

Anne Wheble

AT FLATFORD MILL

Around the millpool, I can see:
      mud
      and leaf
      and tree
      and reed
      and sedge.
That's the grist that the River Stour
Brings to the mill wheel of my mind
At Flatford Mill:
      mud
      and leaf
      and tree
      and reed
      and sedge.
All this is much as John Constable must have seen it;
The trees are taller and the foliage much thicker,
But Willy Lott's white cottage is still there,
Though no washerwoman kneels beside the water
And no dog is on the qui vive in the foreground
And no horse and cart stands stranded in mid-river.
Otherwise everything is much as Constable must have seen it,
And I must look to see it for the first time,
Not painting the scene as Constable might have painted it,
But seeing it all, as he saw it, with an innocent eye.

Stan Downing

A New Dawn

Watch the dawn - her beauty comes
with quiet veils of morning mist,
that kissed the trees.

The bird awakes with song in heart,
they carry on their wing and fly
into the sky to welcome you.

Brenda D Volanthen

SOD'S LAW

He is here again.
My long-lost lover.
Book . . . in hand
And . . . on the cover.
It states . . . Herein, here are my rules.
The ones that work
And . . . make *you* all fools.

Your lives, none of you control, but you
Go always for the hyperbole.
Exaggeration for effect.
Not one of you, got past me yet.

You see . . . all I have to do is wait.
In time . . . you must pass by my gate,
And when you do, I wave my hand,
And . . . chaos reigns.
You're . . . in my land.

Sometimes . . . I give a little peace.
Your pain more felt, when I release
The 'pit falls' within my law book here,
Dismay abounds . . . oh dear, oh dear.

When . . . will I release the *hook*?
Let's see my dear,
I'll take a look.
Oh sorry . . . it's not a finite thing.
After all . . .
My . . . fun's in sin.

All seven exist.
I catch you all
And . . . I have been doing this
Since . . . the fall.

Sheila Mack

A Boy

You who have been born
Announce your arrival
At considerable volume
To us, your adoring public

For now the trials of life
Will be but distant drums
That cause you no distress
But lull you as you slumber

And should their pitch begin
To offend, call on us
Defenders of your claim
To be good, a happy life.

Alan Wilson

MADHOUSE

You have taken to talking to the house plants.
I note you have named the big cactus after me,
And a variegated something or other after your mother -
Might I suggest a nice daisy to cross pollinate with your therapist?

You seem to find it more effortless to be friendly to vegetables -
Exchanging coffee pot pleasantries over your breakfast hangover -
Than to befriend me, with whom, of late,
You share the rooting pot in a rather sodden vegetative state.

And it's very telling, I think,
That you should choose to send your sanity off picking wild flowers
Precisely when the relationship between the cat and I has
                                        reached the point
Where all he does is dig in the flowerbed I've made for myself.

For all you care.

I'm sure his rhododendron namesake would wither immediately
Were you to pepper the soil, even a bit, against him,
Or simply take my side as he's
Remorselessly banging on about me having no respect
                                        for his intelligence,
While he thinks nothing of taking a casual p**s on my work.

No, you just keep weeping over that thorny weed you call mother
While he wraps you that bit further around his little finger.
Paw. Whatever.

Damien Kelly

Never Too Old

(This poem was written two days after the visit when I had
my face painted, for the hell of it, as a tiger.
A woman around my age said, 'Aren't you a bit old for that?'
I replied, 'You're never too old.')

The saddest place I've ever been,
left me feeling pretty damn mean.
I've been sad, even depressed,
melancholy, definitely repressed.

Negative thoughts by the thousand,
have crossed my mind before.
I've even knocked voluntarily,
at death's darkened door.

But the reaper can sod off now,
because I'm all for living, and how!
Anything goes for me and my family,
after a visit, to Eastbourne cemetery.

Danny Coleman

A Tribute To All Voluntary Workers

The folk who work for charity, are of a special breed,
They volunteer their services wherever there's a need.
Though many of mature age, from their working life retired,
They support a chosen charity and do what is required.
Many serve in the various shops, selling donated goods,
Others drive for 'meals on wheels',
Bringing house-bound folk cooked foods.
There's a group known as 'good neighbours' who do household repairs
For the handicapped and elderly, to show that someone cares.
Then there's those who work for hospices, doing what they can
To bring comfort to those who suffer, their less fortunate fellow man.
Every voluntary effort can help in many ways,
Giving aid to those in need, and to brighten up their days.
Well done! To those who give their time, for whichever worthy cause,
In this theatre of life, they deserve a grand applause!

Evelyn Williams

ODE TO CHANTELLE

I first met Chantelle at her interview
what a nervous day all around
but a willing and able teacher
is that day what we found.

She's made her mark at our school
in many more ways than one
and a friend for life we've all made
one we'll miss, when she has gone.

What does she do? How does she relax
after a PTFA meeting?
Well, she's been to concerts and listens to
the gorgeous Ronan Keating!

She's a family girl at heart
for them all, she really does care.
She's proud of her house, loves animals
Tom and her are a matching pair.

But one of the things that I'll remember,
is her ability to mislay things.
Where is it? I just had it!
Round the school, her cry rings!

Now laminating pouches
I think she eats them for her lunch!
She laminates everything she can
of the children's work, she's proud as punch!

But she's lovely and she's happy
she makes us all feel good
especially when things go wrong
and the day's not been so good.

So who will cheer us up?
Who will make us smile?
Oh! Chantelle, I think we'll
miss you for quite a while!

Lynda J Smith

IN WHICH WE ARE BORN

Sometimes from where I sit, or sometimes walk,
of this in life's different ways
this way of life's path we tread each day,
each month, each year in our lives.
What needs in life do we require?
Are there sacred means, we of some do follow,
yet not, not all in day to day will,
yet on hard times, will of sacred ways will follow.
As I sit or walk, sometimes I contemplate, of these ways,
yet never changed our life from day to day.

In life ever fair is this of life we share,
as I walk, this I contemplate of life afar
no changes from day to day are there.
Our wanton ways do bear, of day to day in life's ways,
for what in life is fair, this planet shared,
this I contemplate in life's way.
As I sit or walk, in life's path to be of good cheer,
sometimes life is not all bad.
In certain ways, in life we try to comply,
those ways of life to which we are born
into this planet afar, of that we are apart from day to day.

A May

GROWING UP

When we are children we are shy to everyone we meet.
When we are teenagers we watch everything we eat.
Looking in the mirror, not liking what we see.
Wondering whom on earth is going to fancy me.

When walking down the street not thinking who we are going to meet.
A boy passing by gives you the eye.
Starting to blink, stick your nose in the air.
Give a toss of your hair as if you didn't care.
For now you know with boys on your mind,
That you are no longer a child.

Sylvia Brown

THANK YOU FOR HELPING RATTY

Oh, Environment Agency, you discovered
Ratty of 'The Wind In The Willows'' fame had lost
Most of his relatives, sister, father, mother,
In the last fifteen years. Then he has paid the cost

Of living by streams, to the American Minks.
They'd escaped from fur farms; and squat where Ratty dwells,
Just to spy along back walls, for tell-tale chinks,
Or to sniff flat stones for 'typical water vole' smells.

They made short work of massacring his neighbours -
Without leaving a whisker or tail behind.
Foiling mink, (not before time) will do these voles favours.
Plant reedbeds, please. Make Ratty's door hard to find.

For once, our road improvements will have to cede to
The needs of a vole colony found near Rye.
A re-widening for the main coast road was due -
Until Ratty was seen: and the job stopped thereby.

Gillian Fisher

SEASONS OF LONG AGO

Do you remember springtime in the years so long ago?
When icy air still lingered as we watched the catkins blow.
When pussy willow branches were to nature tables brought,
With the jars of frogspawn, which with friends we'd keenly sought.
When days grew gently warmer and the lambs would all appear,
The daffodils and crocus spoke of Easter drawing near.

Then, of course, came summer with its days of endless sun.
We always had good summers; long, hot days of endless fun.
School was out and holidays were spent beside the sea,
Paddling and jumping waves, and donkey rides and tea.
We'd stroll in summer meadows, to our knees in flowers wild,
Or lie and watch the passing clouds, contented, just a child.

Remember golden, mellow light of autumn-shortened days?
The still of Indian summer's sun held warmth within its rays.
Leaves a blaze of glory to be rustled through at will.
The scent of fruits and plenty bring me hosts of memories still.
But there among the dying year were moments jewel bright;
Harvest home and fireworks, conkers and bonfire night.

So came the blast of wintertime with winds, and ice and snow.
Trees were bare, the ground was hard and nature'd nought to show.
But still there were some high spots, that I can call to mind;
Like Christmas with its magic and folk all being kind.
And wasn't New Year special with its fresh new start to bring;
With hope and resolutions to set full hearts to sing.

We mustn't lose the wonder of that child of long ago;
No matter what the passing years in curse and blessings throw.
Try to keep the hope alive, believe in power of good.
Try to look for positives, not on the darkness brood.
Meet the seasons as they come with all they offer you.
Each one has something special - reminisce, you'll know it's true.

Olwyn Green

ANCHOR BOOKS
SUBMISSIONS INVITED
SOMETHING FOR EVERYONE

ANCHOR BOOKS GEN - Any subject, light-hearted clean fun, nothing unprintable please.

THE OPPOSITE SEX - Have your say on the opposite gender. Do they drive you mad or can we co-exist in harmony?

THE NATURAL WORLD - Are we destroying the world around us? What should we do to preserve the beauty and the future of our planet - you decide!

All poems no longer than 30 lines.
Always welcome! No fee!
Plus cash prizes to be won!

Mark your envelope (eg *The Natural World)*
And send to:
Anchor Books
Remus House, Coltsfoot Drive
Peterborough, PE2 9JX

OVER £10,000 IN POETRY PRIZES
TO BE WON!

Send an SAE for details on our New Year 2002 competition!